Proposals

PROPOSALS

by

Neil Simon

STAGE
&SCREEN
The Book Club for the Performing Arts

Neil Simon's PROPOSALS premiered at the Broadhurst
Theatre on November 6, 1997. It was produced by
Emanuel Azenberg. It was directed by Joe Mantello. The
set designs were by John Lee Beatty, the costume designs
were by Jane Greenwood, the lighting design was by
Brian MacDevitt and the sound design was by Tom Clark.
Incidental music was by Stephen Flaherty. The produc-
tion stage manager was William Joseph Barnes. General
managers were Abbie M. Strassler and John S. Corker.
Technical supervision was provided by Unitech II, Corp.
Press representative was Bill Evans & Associates. Casting
by Jay Binder. Associate producer was Ginger Montel.

THE CAST

(*In order of appearance*)

Clemma Diggins . . . . L. Scott Caldwell

Burt Hines . . . . Dick Latessa

Josie Hines . . . . Suzanne Cryer

Ken Norman . . . . Reg Rogers

Ray Dolenz . . . . Matt Letscher

Annie Robbins . . . . Kelly Bishop

Vinnie Bavasi . . . . Peter Rini

Sammii . . . . Katie Finneran

Lewis Barnett . . . . Mel Winkler

Near a resort in the Pocono Mountains, Pennsylvania

ACT ONE

ACT I

Scene One

The exterior of a charming and modest summer cottage in the Pocono Mountains in Pennsylvania. It's wood and it's old, with a shingle roof and an open porch. There's a single rocking chair and a small swinging sofa for two.

Two steps down and we're on the ground. In front of the house is a large tree trunk, smoothed even on the top surface that serves as a table. It sits in between two rattan chairs on either side.

Foliage is above and around the house. It's been left to grow wild since any effort to tame and trim it usually becomes futile. There is an open space in the wood at stage left that leads to a path. The entrance to the house is unseen because it's at the rear of what we see. Cars drive up and park, which we hear but never see. Besides coming through the house, one can come down a path just to the side of the house.

It is late August and the sun has been down nearly an hour now. The porch light is on and the house lights are on.

Clemma Diggins, an African-American, mid-forties, appears from the path opening at the side. She wears a thin print dress and a loose button sweater that is now open so she can wrap it around her arms to keep her warm. She wears a ribbon in her hair and slippers.

3

She looks at the house as if seeing it anew. She looks up at the sky, and wraps the sweater around her even tighter. When she speaks, it's for the audience's ears, but she seems to be talking more to her inner self.

Clemma: This time of year, I usually think of this house . . . and usually 'bout this time of night . . . this kinda weather too. Just enough to chill your bones and tell you this here summer is 'bout ready to pack up and go into storage for good . . . . I don't rightly know if this house is still standin' . . . If it is, it wouldn't look much different than it does now, 'cause it never changed in the twenty-two summers I spent here. One thing always puzzled me. There's gotta be what, twenty, thirty billion birds in the world? . . . All kindsa birds. They keep gettin' born every minute and dyin' every minute . . . Then how come this place ain't littered with dead birds? They don't live as long as folks do. So you'd think if you stepped outta the house in the mornin', you'd need an umbrella to keep them dead birds from bouncin' off your head. When I worked here for Mr. Burt Hines and his family, we'd do a lotta barbecuin' right over there. Never once saw a dead bird fall into my barbecue sauce . . . Now when *people* die, you know about it. You hear about it. Some relative's gonna call screamin' in the middle of the night about it . . . . See, when my time came, I just slipped away quietly in my bed . . . Most people would pay good money to make their departure in that manner . . . Trouble with dyin' in your sleep is, you never know when you're dead . . . You missed the slippin' away part . . . You're tryin' to wake up in the mornin' and there's no way you can do it . . . I went in my ninety-second year and in my family, that was goin' young . . . . Now the people I worked for, Mr. Hines in particular, was only fifty-five when he got sick and that man was makin' no effort to delay the inevitable.

(*Burt Hines, fifty-five, comes out of the house, looks up at the sky, then looks around to make sure he's alone. Burt crosses to the rattan chair near the tree stump and sits*)

Clemma: Here he goes. Watch this. (*Burt takes a cigarette out of his shirt pocket, puts it in his mouth*) See what I mean? Might as well be puttin' a gun in his mouth. (*Burt takes out a lighter, lights it and takes a puff*)

Clemma: Now one cigarette ain't gonna do it as fast as a bullet . . . But he ain't in no rush. He still got some affairs to put in order before he falls outta the sky into some hole in the ground he already picked out and paid for. Now this all goes back some forty, fifty years ago . . . countin' time the way living folks do . . . . The world was different then . . . some ways better, some ways worse. At the time, I was a Negro . . . could have been Colored, don' remember . . . . Don' know *what* they'd call me today . . . But right now, this night, this minute I am what I was then. Just a hard workin' woman tryin' to save the life of a good lovin' man from fallin' outta the sky before his time. (*She moves slowly to where Burt is standing. He's inhaling his cigarette. Clemma stamps her feet hard at him*) Caught you!! . . . I knew it. I knew

5

if I waited in them bushes long enough, I'd catch you with a cigarette in your mouth.

Burt (*grabs his chest*): Jesus, Clemma. You scared the life out of me.

Clemma: What'd the doctor say to you 'bout smokin' cigarettes? Ain't you had enough heart attacks this year? "It's your life, Mr. Hines," ain't that what he said?

Burt: No. He said smoking wasn't as bad as someone jumping out of the woods at me. I thought you went to bed.

Clemma: Tha's what I told you. But I've been settin' in them bushes waitin' to catch you. (*reaches her hand out*) Give it here now.

Burt: One last puff.

Clemma (*nods*): Tha's what it's gonna be. Your last puff . . . I don' know what you're rushin' to get to heaven for 'cause they don' 'low no smokin' up there anyways. (*he takes one more puff*) Okay. Tha's your last. Hand it over now.

Burt: Stop bossing me, Clemma.

Clemma: Fine with me. But you just remember what I tole you. One more heart attack and I'm quttin'. I'm thirty-seven years old and I got better things to do than watch a man clutchin' his chest and kickin' his feet up in the air.

Burt: You were thirty-seven ten years ago.

Clemma: Tha's right. And I'll be thirty-seven twenty years from now. I got the kinda face that don' age. (*puts hand out again*) Last time before I pack my bags. (*He gives her the cigarette. She crosses as if she's going into the house, but she sits on the porch steps, and takes a drag on the cigarette*) Ain't even got a filter tip. You sure know all the short cuts to the graveyard, don' you?

Burt: I *knew* you were going to do that. You're a worse smoker than I am.

Clemma (*shakes head "no"*): Don' put me in *your* category. I'm just a left over smoker. And you don' leave enough over for a woman to work up a good cough.

Burt: Really? And who's that I hear coughing in your room?

(*Clemma puts out the cigarette on the bottom of her shoe and puts it in her sweater pocket*)

Clemma: Don' worry about my coughin', 'cause this girl ain't dyin' till her ninety-third year.

Burt: Good. Then we'll go together.

Clemma: That's what you *hope*. Mine is guaranteed. The gypsy lady read my palm. (*holds out hand, palm up*) See this. I got a life line so long, it goes up my arm and *all* the way down my leg.

Burt: I had my palm read once. The woman told me I was going to have a great career in the entertainment business.

Clemma: There you are. She tole you the truth, didn't she?

Burt: Retailing television sets is not a great career in the entertainment business.

Clemma: You jus' look at the negative all the time. All you Jewish men do that . . . You don' talk to God enough, that's your trouble.

Burt: Maybe you're right. I just get lazy about it. How about if I go to church with you some Sunday morning.

Clemma: Uh uh. No, sir. God din' go to the trouble makin' you Jewish jus' to come to my church and take up a seat . . . I like Jewish people . . . the prayin' is good but the cookin'll kill you.

Burt (*crossing to her, hugs her*): I really love you, Clemma. Always have. I hope that doesn't make you nervous.

Clemma: You ain't in no condition to make me nervous.

Burt: You just wait and see. I'll dance at Josie's wedding . . . with you.

Clemma: If there *is* a wedding.

Burt: What do you mean? Don't you think that Kenny and Josie are going to get married?

Clemma: Ain't none of my business.

Burt: Sure it is. You're the one she confides in, not Mrs. Hines.

Clemma: Mrs. Who?

Burt: Sorry. Mrs. *Robbins*. We've been divorced three years and I still make that mistake.

Clemma: Only mistake you made was lettin' that woman go in the first place. Never once saw you clutchin' your chest when you two was married.

Burt: You still didn't tell me what you think of Josie marrying Kenny.

Clemma: She ain't *gonna* marry him.

Burt: They're engaged. Did she tell you she won't marry him?

Clemma: Don' have to. I been holdin' that girl in my arms since day one. I see the way she looks at him.

Burt: How?

Clemma: She looks at him engaged. But she don' look at him married. It's gettin' cold. I'm goin' in. You get inside if you know what's good for you.

Burt: I've got a sweater on.

Clemma: Ain't no trouble for the mortician to take it off.

(*She goes into the house*)

(*Josie Hines appears. Maybe out of breath but not out of shape. She is twenty-three, wearing shorts, sneakers, no socks, and her father's shirt.*

She has an athletic body, brimming with health and vitality. She's pretty with a determined and intelligent face. She is carrying a long stick she found in the woods)

Josie: What were you and Clemma talking about?

Burt: Marriage.

Josie (*nods*): You two planning to elope?

Burt: No . . . is that what you and Kenny are planning?

Josie (*she looks away*): Hardly.

Burt: Where is he?

Josie: Back there. He's coming.

Burt: What's wrong Josie?

Josie: Would you think I was terrible if I broke my engagement to Kenny?

(*He turns, looks back at door where Clemma went in, then back to Josie*)

Burt: No. But I'd be surprised . . . What happened?

Josie: Are you ready for a surprise?

Burt: Is that what you did? (*She nods*) Just now? (*She nods*) In the woods? (*She nods*) I'm sorry.

Josie: Oh, God, Dad. I feel so awful.

Burt: Well, it's not an easy thing to tell anyone.

Josie: You should have seen his face. You can't imagine how hurt he was.

Burt: I guess I can.

Josie: Oh, no. I'm so sorry. I wasn't thinking. Sometimes I wonder whose genes I got and it scares me.

Burt: You don't just get one parent's genes. If I just got my mother's, I'd be five-foot-two and worried why no one's eating. (*He looks around for Kenny*) Is Kenny okay?

Josie: I don't think so . . . Would you talk to him?

Burt: And tell him what?

Josie: That I'm not worth it.

Burt: Who would ever believe you're not worth it?

Josie: How could Mom be so dumb as to leave someone like you?

Burt: Because I was dumb enough to let it happen.

(*Ken Norman enters from the woods. He looks bedraggled. He's mid-twenties, a little Brooks Brothers but attractive and right now, fighting despair*)

Kenny (*surprised to see Burt*)**:** Oh. Hello, Mr. Hines.

Burt: Oh, Kenny. Hi . . . Hi . . . God, I suddenly feel chilly . . . You feel chilly, Ken?

Ken: No.

Burt: Josie?

Josie: No.

Burt: Well, that's 'cause you're young. Young takes care of everything. Trust me, Kenny . . . Well, I'm going in. It's getting chilly. Goodnight.

(*He goes in*)

Josie (*to Kenny*)**:** You okay?

Kenny: Okay? . . . Oh, yeah . . . yes . . . I'm okay . . . I'm fine . . . I really am . . . No. I'm not okay . . . I will be . . . one day.

Josie (*nods. Doesn't know what to say*)**:** Kenny?

Kenny: What?

Josie: Would you like a beer?

Kenny: Instead of getting married? No.

Josie: Well. I think that's what I need right now.

(She gets up. She looks at him, wanting to say something. She can't, turns and goes into the house.

He picks up her stick, looks at it, swishes it a couple of times, then in a quick fury, he breaks the stick over his knee, then breaks it again and tosses the pieces into the woods.

Josie comes out with a bottle of beer. She drinks from it)

Josie: God, I really love beer. One day I'm going to get so fat from drinking this.

Kenny: Yeah, right.

Josie: No, I am. I'm going to get big fat hips like I'm carrying tennis balls in my pockets. And big jowls hanging down. And little piggy eyes and nubby knees and I'm going to have to wear Hawaiian dresses the rest of my life.

Kenny: Is that what you want me to think, Josie? That you're going to blow up to two hundred and eighty pounds? Fine with me. Let's get married and I'll buy bigger furniture.

Josie (*dismisses it, looks around*): Where's my stick? Did you see my stick?

Kenny: No.

Josie: Really? I left it right here.

Kenny: I broke it.

Josie: You broke my stick? Why?

Kenny: Because it was *my* time to break something.

Josie: Oh. It's okay. I don't blame you for hating me.

Kenny: *Hate* you? I love you. I loved you from the first time I saw you.

Josie: What I meant is. I'm the one who broke off the engagement and for that, you have every right to hate me.

Kenny: Sorry to disappoint you, but I don't . . . I hate *life*. I hate the *world*. I hate *mankind*. I hate every living creature that crawls and flies, but I'm not through loving you yet.

(*She reaches out and rubs the top of his hand*)

Josie: Kenny, the one thing I hope we'll always be—

Kenny: PLEASE! Don't say friends—I have no interest in the smile or scent of my friends.

Josie: I'm sorry.

Kenny: The thing is, if you wanted to break it off, why did you wait so long?

Josie: I didn't. I wrote you a letter two months ago at school.

Kenny: That wasn't a letter. That was a poem. Where did it say, "Break off the engagement"?

Josie: It said it in the poetry. In the imagery. In metaphors. Did you read it?

Kenny: Yes. "Brazen idols, black damask cheek. Catatonic smiles who cannot speak." That's how you break off with Shelley or Keats. I'm a law student.

Josie: I wrote other letters but never sent them. I thought it was too cowardly not to say it face to face.

Kenny: Except it wasn't face to face. You were standing behind me and you poked me with a stick. "Would you mind awfully, Ken, if we didn't met married?" . . . Poke poke . . . "Would I mind awfully?" . . . What's that supposed to be, polite? Did your mother teach you, "whenever breaking off an engagement, always stand behind the gentleman and poke him gently with a stick and say, 'Would you mind awfully?' " . . . Poke poke.

Josie: I'm sorry. It just came out.

Kenny: No, no. I saw you looking for a stick. Why a stick?

Josie: I was trying to get your attention.

Kenny: *"Would you mind awfully if we didn't get married?"* got my attention . . . you didn't *need* a stick. (*Rubs his neck*)

Josie: It was a bad choice.

Kenny: Why today Josie? Why didn't you tell me before?

Josie: I'm not sure. I guess I was waiting until I was absolutely clear that getting married would be a big mistake for us . . . God, this is hard, Kenny. I care for you. I do. I really have strong feelings for you.

Kenny: I just don't know why you said yes. If you meant "no," how could you have said "yes"?

Josie: Because it seemed right at the time. I thought you were wonderful, Kenny. I still do. You're so smart. So involved with things. Political things. Causes. Things you care about. And you have such great parents. And your mother is incredible. I'm closer to her than I am to my own mother. And I just got swept up by it all . . . So when you suddenly said while we were dancing at the Democratic Convention, "Let's get engaged," I thought, "Swell. What a great guy to be engaged to" . . . I guess I never really thought about it leading up to marriage.

Kenny: What'd you *think* it would lead up to? More Democratic Conventions?

Josie: I just loved being with you. Until I finally realized something was wrong. I was enjoying living *your* life. I was forgetting about living mine.

Kenny: Then forget mine. It's not important. I can live mine in my spare time.

Josie: When my mother left my father, he was devastated. He loved her. He still does. I realize that's not the same because they had twenty-one years together . . . But even with all that, he found that time heals. That you move on. And he's learned to accept that.

Kenny: Gee, *that* story certainly perked me up. So now I know what I have to look forward to—acceptance.

Josie: No. You have your *life* to look forward to.

Kenny: Can't you just hold off your decision until the end of the summer?

Josie: Nothing will change.

Kenny: I wish I could have been born your brother.

Josie: Why?

Kenny: So I'd always be around you . . . but if I was your brother and you loved me the way I wanted you to, that would really be sick . . . so forget that one.

Josie: I do love you. In my own way. (*She puts her arms around him, hugs him*)

Kenny: If I had one wish in the world, I would . . . (*he catches himself about to cry, walks away*) I wasn't crying. I'm saving that for the trip back home.

Josie: You want me to drive you home?

Kenny: Oh. The final humiliation. Drop me off in front of my mother who's writing out the invitations.

Josie: What are you going to tell her?

Kenny: I'll have my father tell her. She never listens to what he says anyway. (*He looks at her*) I'll just love you for another few months . . .and then I'll try to cut down (*He starts to go*)

Josie: Kenny, wait! (*He turns, looks at her*) I have to give your ring back. (*She starts to loosen it*)

Kenny: No! Don't! Not while I'm watching. (*He turns and goes*)

(*Josie sits on the swing chair, upset with herself. Burt comes out in pajamas, robe, and slippers*)

Burt: I wish I had another daughter.

Josie: Oh, God. You were listening?

Burt: I tried not to . . . I failed. (*He sits next to her*)

Josie: You think I handled it alright?

Burt: Well, you could have done without the stick.

Josie: How did you feel when Mom said she was leaving you?

Burt: Like a train ran over me . . .then backed up and ran over me again.

Josie: Sounds like Mom. Barreling down the tracks, tooting her own whistle.

Burt: Don't be too tough on her, Josie. Except for leaving me, she's one terrific woman.

Josie: You never say a word against her, do you?

Burt: I can't help it. I still sleep in the same bed she used to sleep in. Unfortunately, she won't tomorrow night. She's coming up.

Josie (*looks at him, surprised*): I thought she was in Paris . . . Don't tell me you called her there?

Burt: Alright, I won't.

Josie: Something's up. You wouldn't have asked her to fly in from Paris unless it's important—are you telling me everything?

Burt: No. Why should I tell you everything?

Josie: I don't keep secrets from you.

Burt: You don't have to. I eavesdrop.

Josie: God. I know just how she's going to look, exactly what she's going to wear.

Burt: What?

Josie: Your favorite dress. All the jewelry you ever gave her. The perfume she doesn't wear anymore but will tomorrow just for you. It's so calculated. So manipulative. She likes coming on to you.

Burt: Why would she come on to me? She's very happy with Walter.

Josie: Because she wants you to still be in love with her. I know. Because there's a part of me that wants Kenny to keep on loving me. Isn't that the worst thing you ever heard?

Burt: No. Just the most honest. None of us ever wants to stop being loved. (*He gets up quickly. Rubs his hands*) Go get your gear. We're going fishing.

Josie: Now? At night? Clemma would kill me if she knew I took you out.

Burt: She won't know. She's busy on smoke alert. You get the poles, I'll get the tackle.

Josie: You're so bad. (*He goes into the house, Josie gets the poles, Clemma comes out of the house*)

Clemma: What's goin' on here? (*Josie quickly hides the poles*) Somethin' wrong. I can feel it.

Josie: Nothing's wrong, Clemma.

Clemma: Don' tell me. I don' wake up for somethin' goin' right . . . Where's your daddy?

Josie: Gone back to sleep, I guess.

Clemma: Somethin' bad happened. Or somethin' bad's *gonna* happen. You know I'm right, girl.

Josie: I broke off my engagement with Kenny.

Clemma: No, that ain't it. (*She looks around suspiciously*)

Josie: And my mother's coming tomorrow.

Clemma: THERE IT IS! Tha's what's gonna happen . . . he called her, din't he?

Josie: Yes. How'd you know?

Clemma: He's had that Paris phone call look in his eye lately. Oh. You got one while you were disengagin' with Kenny.

Josie: Who was it?

Clemma: The one you tole me you met in Miami. The one you danced with. The one your momma hated.

Josie: Oh, my God. Vinnie Bavasi? What's he want?

Clemma: He'll tell you himself. He's drivin' up tomorrow.

Josie: He's coming here? You said yes without asking me?

Clemma: He din't ask me either. He makes up your mind for you. Sounds like riff raff to me. Talks to you like he's holdin' up a gas station . . . . What you foolin' around with someone like that for, girl?

Josie: I didn't fool around with him. I had one dance with him to spite my mother.

Clemma: Spitin' your momma ain't gonna help. If she hated him in Miami, she's gonna *de*-test him up here. Now come in before you wake up your Daddy. That man needs his rest.

(*She goes into the house. Burt comes around side of the house*)

Burt: (*keeps low and whispers*): So what do we do about this Bavasi boy?

Josie (*whispers as well*): God, you hear everything. (*She gives him the bait box. She gets the poles*)

Burt: Can't we head him off?

Josie: Vinnie? You'd need a road block . . . Listen, if Clemma hears us, this was your idea.

Burt: Don't worry. Once she gets into bed, she snores like a buzzsaw.

(*They start off*)

Clemma (*from in the house*): *I heard that!* I ain't asleep. (*They run off. Clemma comes out with a torch light. Swings it around to where they just ran off*)

Clemma (*shouts*): Girl!! You come back here! . . . You takin' a sick man out on the lake, you broke off an engagement, and you got a gangster comin' up. (*Shouts louder*) *Ain't you done enough for one day??*

(*The lights dim. Music under the scene change*)

ACT 1

Scene Two

The next morning, about nine thirty. A bright, sunny day.

Josie in a stain splattered shirt, is working on a clay bust, which sits on a stand. It's a head but not yet detailed. It has neither gender nor age.

Clemma comes out in a light print dress. She carries a string shopping bag. She looks out of sorts, She puts a piece of paper and a pencil in front of Josie.

Clemma (*looking away*): Put down what you need for lunch. I ain't talkin' to you.

Josie: What did I do?

Clemma: I heard him sneezin' out there. That man caught everything but fish.

Josie: He had the time of his life. He was happy last night, Clem.

Clemma: He's happy 'cause your momma's comin' up today.

Josie: When did that ever improve things? (*Still working the bust*)

Clemma: Hope is hope, girl. I don' care *who* delivers it.

Josie: God! Vinnie Bavasi and Mom on the same day. Garbo meets Scarface.

Clemma: Scarface?

Josie: His family is Mafia. They all talk like they were punched in the throat, including his mother.

Clemma (*looks at bust*): Girl, sometimes you scare me. Who's that one supposed to be?

Josie: I don't know yet.

Clemma: Whyn't you make it look like your momma? Make a nice present for your daddy.

Josie: My mother? I don't have enough clay for her earrings. . . .

Clemma: You're lucky you ain't my child 'cause I wouldn't let you talk 'bout me like that.

Josie: If I were your child, I wouldn't have to. . . .

Clemma: Well you ain't so you can't . . . Now what about lunch? I count four people including Scar-face.

Josie: Don't count me. I'll be out fishing all day.

Clemma: Well, you better take them folks with you 'cause they ain't comin' to see me.

Josie: Oh. Alright. Four people. And make Dad a special treat.

Clemma: Meaning chili and beans which your momma hates.

Josie: Oh? I didn't know.

Clemma: Honey, you better go to lyin' school 'cause you can't tell the truth worth a damn.

Josie: I'm sorry, but I just don't know how to make everyone happy.

Clemma (*puts note in her pocket*): Josie, you got everythin' a young woman your age could want. You're smart and you're pretty and you're kind to creatures. But you're missin' one thing, honey.

Josie: What's that?

Clemma: Harmony.

Josie: You mean like grits?

Clemma: No, you ignorant child. That's *hominy*. I'm talkin' *harmony* here. Like music in tune. And when you get it in your life, then you have people in tune. And sometimes you're just outta tune, child.

Josie: Oh. And I suppose you're perfect.

Clemma: I never said to be like me. I made more mistakes than a blind race horse . . . But tha's me. You is you . . . I'm goin' marketin'.

(*Clemma turns and starts to walk away. She stops and suddenly grabs her chest and moans slightly*)

Josie (*sees her*): CLEMMA! What's wrong?

(*She rushes to her. Clemma sits slowly on the tree stump*)

Clemma: I got an extra pumpin' feelin' in my chest.

Josie: I'll get you some water. (*But before she can go, Clemma grabs her wrist and holds it tightly*)

Clemma: Don' need no water. Not after brandy, I don'.

Josie: You had brandy this early in the morning?

Clemma: You ain't the only one who's got guests comin' . . . Lewis called me this morning.

Josie: Lewis? Your ex-husband?

Clemma: He ain't ex. He's just been gone for seven years. Just hearin' his voice and I went straight for your daddy's brandy . . . there's no way or reason I want to see him . . . but he's comin' today.

Josie: Today?? With my mother and Vinnie Bavasi?

Clemma: No. He's comin' by himself.

(*The telephone in the house rings*)

Josie: You think he wants to get back with you?

Clemma: Get back? All that man wants is to borrow my life's savings.

27

Josie: Why would you think that?

Clemma: When a man's gone seven years, he don' come back 'cause he thinks you got young and skinny.

(*Burt opens front door, looks out*)

Burt: Josie! Kenny's calling.

Josie: Damn. Tell him I'll call back.

Burt: You'd better take it. He sounds awful.

Josie: So does everybody. Clemma's not feeling well. Just watch her. (*She rushes inside*)

Burt: It's awfully hot, Clem. Why don't you call the grocers and tell them to deliver?

Clemma: I don't buy what I can't see, smell, or squeeze. (*She gets up, starts off. Stops*) Oh. I took a pinch of your brandy this mornin'.

Burt: Oh? Okay. Fine.

Clemma: In that case, I took two pinches.

(*She continues off just as a young man comes up. His name is Ray Dolenz. He's mid-twenties, he's athletic, attractive, and bright. He's also a little hot under the collar*)

Ray: Oh. Hi, Clemma. (*She stops, looks at him*) It's Ray. From the golf club.

Clemma: I know who you are . . . you comin' for lunch too?

Ray: Me? No. I wasn't invited.

Clemma: That hasn't stopped nobody else.

(She leaves. Burt has picked up his golf putter, just holding it)

Burt: Hi, Ray. You just up visiting?

Ray: No. Came back to work at the club. Ran a little short of money. Is Josie here?

Burt *(practices his putting swing)*: She's on the phone.

Ray: Did I hear you're not playing golf this year?

Burt: No, I'm playing. Just not with a ball. How's your book coming? Josie told me Random House took an option.

Ray: Yeah. They just want me to fix up some things.

Burt *(nods)*: Uh huh.

Ray: Everything but the title . . . . Is that a long distance call?

Burt: No. It's Kenny. Have you seen him today?

Ray: I just left him.

Burt: Then you know about—

Ray: Yeah. It's gotten around.

(*Josie comes out of the house*)

Josie: Dad, Kenny's father wants to speak to you.

Burt: Really? I can't imagine why. (*He starts up steps*) Ray's back.

(*Burt goes in*)

Josie: Hi, Ray. I thought I heard your voice.

Ray (*perfunctory*): Hi.

Josie: Kenny told me you were here. The club needs you. Even *I* can beat the pro they have now. Spot me four holes and we can play sometime.

Ray: No, thanks. I'm not sure I'd trust your score-card.

Josie: Oh, great. A hostile golf pro. Probably won't be a big year for tips.

(*She moves over to her sculptured head, picks up some clay*)

Ray (*takes a letter out of his back pocket*): Do you know what this is? Do you have any idea at all?

Josie (*puts clay on bust*): An apology for your last remark?

Ray: It's a suicide note from Kenny. *A god damn suicide note.*

Josie (*stops what she's doing*): Really? And he asked you to deliver it? Does he intend to do it at lunch because he just invited himself over?

Ray: The point is not that he would actually *do* anything. The point is that he's devastated enough to sit down and write this thing.

Josie (*puts down clay*): May I see it?

Ray (*pulls it away*): Do you think I would humiliate my best friend by showing anyone his suicide note?

Josie: He showed it to *you.*

Ray: I pulled it out of the typewriter before he was finished.

Josie: Ray, I'm not going to get overwrought about someone who writes a suicide note with his best friend reading over his shoulder.

Ray: I was at the golf club. Got a message from him. "Come over, it's important." I walked in, he was typing . . . I sat there, he asked me for a synonym for "eternity."

Josie: You *helped* him write this letter?

Ray: What is with you? You seem to be taking this pretty jauntily.

Josie: *Jauntily*? I love your carefully chosen descriptive adverbs, Ray. No. Not jauntily. I'm taking this miserably. I am concerned with Kenny's pain and my guilt. I'm concerned that I hurt somebody I care for . . . But I'm not at *all* interested in what you think, she said *jauntily*.

Ray (*laughs sardonically*): Why am I even talking to you? And why would Kenny want to kill himself over you? I wouldn't nick myself shaving for you.

Josie: And yet you shaved.

Ray: Can we limit this conversation to my friend Kenny?

Josie: Certainly. You know your limitations.

(*She continues sculpting*)

Ray (*tries to put his anger under control*): Kenny Norman is second in his class at Harvard Law and you treat him like shit. He could easily be *first* at Harvard Law but he hates to flaunt his intelligence. He has a soul. He has integrity and a social and political conscience that wouldn't occur to you in a thousand years. He's one of the most decent human beings I ever met. And he'll be important one day. He deserves a woman with as much sensitivity, loyalty, and compassion as he has . . . So how the *hell* can you suddenly, without warning, break off the engagement?

Josie: Ray, instead of assassinating my character, why don't you take the day off and look for someone with more sensitivity, loyalty, and compassion than me. And *I'll* go give the golf lessons.

Ray: Putting a golf club in your hands would be lethal. I would hate to take a 'poke poke' with a five iron.

Josie: Oh. Is that the only part he mentioned?

Ray: Would you like to hear the rest? He described it as, "like getting a Dear John letter from a tree."

Josie: Did he send you here? Or are you just miserable because you had to come back to a job you hate?

Ray: You think he sent me? You really don't know him, do you? And certainly not like I do. His parents practically raised me. Kenny got me this job. His father helped to get me into Brown University. Kenny and I are blood brothers. He gave me his blood when I was in my car accident two years ago. You understand?

Josie: I don't care if Kenny personally breastfed you. I don't have to defend myself to you.

(*She starts for the house*)

Ray: Is there a chance you might change your mind?

Josie (*she stops*): How interesting . . . That was the same question I asked last summer when someone told *me* it was all over.

Ray (*looks at her, surprised*): Can we stick to current relationships, please?

Josie: Sorry. I didn't mean to make you uncomfortable. No. There's no chance I'm going to change my mind. How does that sit with you?

Ray: I think you're missing out on a terrific guy.

Josie: I had pretty much the same feeling.

Ray: Josie don't.

Josie: Kenny never knew about us, did he? Why didn't you tell him? He didn't have any interest in me then.

Ray: What was there to tell? We had a nice summer flirtation, that's all.

Josie: The only difference between me and Kenny and me and you, is that I *know* why it didn't work with Kenny. You walked out just when it was getting good.

Ray: Getting good didn't mean it was going far. It stopped because it had no future.

Josie: I didn't ask for a future. I was really happy with the present.

Ray: I had a book to write.

Josie: It was going well with the book when it was going well with us.

Ray: You don't get any credit for my book, Josie. Nor any blame when I went cold on it. I'm late for a lesson.

Josie: You gave me up for Kenny, didn't you?

Ray: Oh, come on.

Josie: Was I the payoff for his father getting you into Brown?

Ray: You can't accept a simple rejection, can you?

Josie: Oh, you idiot. If you had stayed with me, Kenny would be engaged to some law student and your book would be in its fifth printing by now.

Ray: Will you stop rewriting life? . . . You don't push characters around anywhere you please. Not everyone has happy endings.

Josie: Who says life is always right? Sometimes people have to give it a shove.

Ray: No matter who gets hurt?

Josie: *Everybody* gets hurt. It's the ones who bounce back that interest me.

Ray: It's the ones who play fair that interest me.

Josie: Can't we *both* be right?

Ray: Not on the same day. Today is Kenny's day to be right.

Josie: Fine. Then look me up tomorrow.

Ray: No, thank you. This is my last visit. And I shaved, because *I* . . . am a very neat guy. (*He turns to go, turns back*) . . . he said tauntingly.

(*A big grin on his face, in triumph, and he goes. Josie stands there feeling a little empty. Burt sticks his head out of an upstairs window*)

Burt: I wasn't listening . . . but can I say something?

Josie: No.

Burt: It's not advice.

Josie: I don't need any.

Burt: I like that Ray . . . I like him a lot.

Josie: Good. Then call him. He's available.

(*She goes in*)

Burt (*shouts down*): *Everyone* around here is available. (*He goes back in*)

(*Lights down. Music in the change.*)

ACT I

Scene Three

Burt is sitting off at the side, a sun reflector to his face, his eyes closed facing the sun.

Clemma comes off the path, her bag filled with groceries. She sees Burt.

Clemma: Do I smell smoke again or is that your face burnin' up?

Burt: Just want to took my best today.

Clemma: You people put so much importance in how you look. (*Mimicking*) "My, don' you look nice" . . . "Aren't you lookin' sweet. Mm mm" . . . "You're gettin' younger every day" . . . You all *know* you're lyin' so what's the point to it?

Burt: Don't you like to hear people say you're looking good?

Clemma: Oh, yeah, but with me, they mean it. The freezer in the store broke down las' night. They won't have meat or chicken till five o'clock, but for lunch, you're gonna see everythin' that can possibly be done with tuna fish.

Burt: Whatever you make will be fine, Clem.

Clemma: Maybe fine for *your* guests but my guest was countin' on ribs.

Burt: I didn't know you *had* a guest.

Clemma: Didn' Josie tell you?

Burt (*gets up*): Josie never tells me anything. I have to hear it through the window. Who's your guest?

Clemma: Lewis.

Burt: Your Lewis? I'll be glad to see him. I always liked him.

Clemma: Tha's 'cause you were smart enough not to marry him.

Burt: What's he been doing all these years?

Clemma: I could guess but I ain't a swearin' kinda woman.

Burt: You nervous about seeing him?

Clemma: You nervous 'bout seein' Mrs. Robbins?

(*They look at each other and both laugh together*)

Clemma: Then you and I oughta go inside and finish that brandy.

(*We hear a car horn honk twice*)

Clemma: Tha's her. Two honks on the horn. You got 'bout twenty seconds to get yourself some more tan on your face.

(*Josie rushes out*)

Josie: Her car is pulling up. I can hear her pearls jiggling.

Clemma: You be nice to her, you hear me. She's still your Momma.

(*She goes inside*)

Annie (*offstage*): Helloo? Burt? Josie? It's mother.

Josie: Right. Like we couldn't tell from the perfume.

Burt (*to Josie*): Josie, for my sake, you be nice to her.

Josie: Can I at least grit my teeth?

(*Annie Robbins appears. She is about forty-seven and attractive. She is smartly dressed, showing a still trim figure. She wears jewelry that seems a bit unusual for a weekend in the country*)

Annie: Oh, you're all out here. My God, it's so hot. I forgot about this place in August. Burt, are you alright in this weather?

Burt: Yes. Now that a fresh breeze just blew in.

Annie: Oh, that's sweet. (*She kisses him*) I like being called a fresh breeze. And how's my Josie?

Josie (*sitting at sculpting table*): Fine, now that a fresh mother just blew in . . . . How was Paris, Mom?

Annie: Beautiful but hot. Their idea of air conditioning is to open a window.

Burt: The heat never bothered you when we were there on our honeymoon.

Annie: No, because it rained every day.

Burt: Really? I never noticed.

Clemma: MR. HINES! TWELVE O'CLOCK!

Burt: I'll be right back. It's time for my pill. And as I recall, you never noticed either.

(*He goes inside*)

Annie: Well, he *seems* chipper. (*Opens her arms*) Come here, honey. Wipe your hands and give me a hug.

(*Josie crosses and they embrace*)

Josie (*holding up hands*)**:** Okay? Didn't leave a mark on you.

Annie: No, no. I've been in Europe for six weeks. I need a kiss. (*She holds Josie and kisses her cheek. Josie pulls away*) Wait! I got lipstick on your face.

Josie: No, Mom, that's the kiss from last year.

Clemma: I knew you'd be needin' something like this. (*They hug*) Good to see you, Mrs. Robbins.

Annie: Oh, Clemma. Your lemonade. That's all I could think of on the road. I knew you'd have some ready. How have you been?

Clemma: Oh, I'm fine. And don't you look good. You're lookin' real fine, Mrs. Robbins. Mm hmm. Ain't your mother lookin' sweet, Josie? Lookin' younger every day.

Annie (*to Clemma*): Oh, please. I put on two pounds in Paris.

Josie (*working on clay*): We know, mother. It was in the *New York Times*.

(*Clemma nudges Josie*)

Annie: You don't have to nudge her, Clemma. Josie thinks all her jokes go over my head.

Clemma: Don' mind her, Mrs. Robbins. She's just excited 'bout seein' you. (*She glares at Josie*) Well, I got eight cans a tuna fish in there just waitin' for me to get some inspiration (*Starts for house*) Oh. D'ja see what Josie's makin', Mrs. Robbins? That's gonna be your face. She's workin' *real hard* on it. (*She glares at Josie and goes in*)

Annie: What a nice surprise, Josie.

Josie (*nods, smiles*): Yeah. For me too.

Annie: Well, let me look at you. Is this a happy girl I see? Heh? Things are going great with you and Kenny. I could tell the minute I saw you.

41

Josie: Amazing how well you know me.

Annie: I always did, didn't I? (*Looks up, squints eyes*) I've got to get out of the sun. What am I going to do with these little crows feet around the eyes?

Josie: You can buy little *slippers* for them.

Annie: Be kind to me, Josie. Your mother is getting old.

Josie: Oh, Mother. Your skin is so well protected, a safecracker couldn't get through . . . You look great.

(*She covers her sculpture with wet rags*)

Annie: I do? Thank you. Do you think your dad thinks so?

Josie: Why is it so important for him to think so?

Annie (*looks at her*): I don't know how to answer that. It just is . . . So, if I may change the subject, have you and Kenny chosen the big day?

Josie: Well, actually it was yesterday.

Annie: Yesterday? You got married *yesterday*?

Josie: Not quite. I broke it off yesterday.

Annie: You broke what off? The *engagement*?

Josie: I decided it would be a mistake for both of us.

Annie: Oh, Josie, I feel so badly. For both of you. And for his family . . . Have you heard from them yet?

Josie: Well, his father called and his best friend delivered a suicide note.

Annie: His best friend wants to commit suicide?

Josie: No. Kenny wrote it.

Annie: Kenny did? Is he that despondent?

Josie: I don't think so. It's just his way of working things out.

Annie: Are *you* alright, Josie?

Josie: Yes. I'm fine . . . No. I'm *not* fine. But it's something I had to do.

Annie: I wish we could have talked first.

Josie: It wouldn't have changed anything.

Annie: It must have been awful telling him.

Josie: Yes . . . Well, you know how that is.

Annie (*recoils from that dig*): Yes. I do. Thank you for reminding me. (*She walks away*)

Josie: I'm sorry. It's a little early in the day to have said that.

Annie: No, no. I'm used to it by now.

Josie: It was stupid and arrogant and I'm sorry. It's just a dangerous subject for you and I to get into . . . Inasmuch as I'm accusing you of the same crime I've just committed.

Annie: Well, when you can stop thinking of it as a crime, maybe it'll be a subject we can get into. (*She turns away*) God, what I'd give for a cigarette right now.

Clemma: Josie. He's on the phone again.

Josie: Kenny?

Clemma: No. The bossy one from Miami. He's down the hill askin' for directions.

Josie: Why didn't you give them to him?

Clemma: I don' know how to drive here. I sit in back of the car comin' up and goin' home on Labor Day. That's the only directions I know.

Annie: Tell him it's the third turnoff on the right after the intersection.

Clemma: I din' know that. No one ever tole me that. (*She goes back in*)

Annie (*to Josie*): Who's coming from Miami?

Josie: Vinnie Bavasi . . . The one I danced with when we were down there. (*Annie shrugs, can't remember*) Black hair, pointy shoes, yellow sports shirt. He came over to our table, asked me to dance. You looked at him and covered up your jewelry.

Annie (*she covers her necklace*): Oh, my God. You're still seeing him?

Josie: I *never* saw him. I danced with him. Once . . . He just invited himself up. I thought he'd be dead by now.

Annie: I hope Kenny doesn't hear about this.

Josie: He probably will. He's coming to lunch.

Annie: To lunch? After writing a suicide note?

Josie (*nods*): With Vinnie. Who knows? Maybe Ray'll pop in too.

Annie: Ray? From last summer? (*Josie nods*) I though that was all over with.

Josie: So did I. So did he. But he was just here and he called me a shit and suddenly it felt kind of good again.

Annie: Does your father know about this?

Josie: Yes. He listens to my life through the window.

Annie: Has he said anything to you?

Josie: Yes. He said, "Don't close the window."

Annie: Don't you think this is a lot for him to deal with? In his condition?

Josie: His condition?

Annie: You know what I'm talking about. His health.

Josie: Oh. Well, his health is lousy but his condition is fine. He's having a real good summer. Obviously not as good as other summers but he fishes a little and we walk some and he laughs a lot. He just likes being with his family. Me and Clemma.

Annie (*she turns, walks away*): Josie, if you want to hurt me, I'll meet you in the city and you can do it there. But not here. And not today. Give your father this weekend, will you?

Josie: I give him *every* weekend . . . But, yes, this *is* a special weekend. Because you're here. He still loves you, you know. Well, of course you do . . . And he'll have you until tomorrow afternoon. And then you'll fly off to Paris or Rome or wherever your husband is waiting for you. So I hope you'll understand if I get upset when you start to talk to me about his condition.

Annie: I understand perfectly. And I am not asking for understanding when I tell you I never walked away from this situation scot free. I pay for it every day of my life. Especially the days when I talk to you. That is *my* condition. And I will deal with that in my own way. What bothers me is our condition, our relationship. I am still part of *your* family. And I don't know how to get back in. I need some help from you. Do you know how we can do that?

Josie: No.

Annie: Are you saying you're turning your back on me?

Josie: No. I'm saying it sincerely. I hate what's happening between us. But I'm telling you I don't know how to make it better.

Annie: Well, then, we'll have to find a way, won't we? . . . I'm going in. I need to wash off seventeen hours of TWA.

(*She turns to go*)

Josie: Mom? If you have a minute, would you talk to Clemma? She's had a bad morning. Lewis is coming today.

Annie: Lewis? After all these years he's coming *today*? . . . Is this some national holiday I forgot about?

Josie: Would you? She really respects you.

Annie: Of course . . . Funny how everyone's converging today. I should have checked my horoscope this morning.

(*She goes into the house. Ray appears suddenly*)

Ray: I am *not* here because I want to be here.

Josie: You never are. So why are you here?

Ray: To warn you. Kenny heard you have some guy coming over for lunch today and he hit the ceiling. If he sees this guy, he's going to nail him.

Josie: Nail Vinnie? I wouldn't advise it. Vinnie has a *mother* who could handle Kenny.

Ray: Can't you call off the lunch?

Josie: No, I can't. I could possibly have stopped the Russian *Revolution* but not this lunch. I didn't ask my mother to come, I didn't invite Vinnie. Kenny invited himself. Clemma has to deal with her husband who suddenly shows up after seven years, Surprise Surprise . . . I'm not getting along all that well with my mother and you're only talking to me out of some weird sense of loyalty to a guy whose father got you into Brown . . . NO! I CANNOT STOP THIS LUNCH!

Ray (*shrugs it off easily*): Okay . . . Fine. Point made. Sorry I bothered you.

(*He starts to go*)

Josie (*moves after him*): Why do you walk away every time there's a problem with us?

Ray (*amused*): Because there's always a problem with us. Look, I made my pitch about Kenny. I don't care about Vinnie. My best to your father and good luck to Clemma and her husband. Ray, is now leaving, so goodbye.

(*He turns, starts away. Josie moves after him again*)

Josie: Who is she?

Ray (*turns back to her*): Did I leave someone out? Who?

Josie: The girl you're seeing in New York.

Ray (*amused again*): Who told you about her?

Josie: Kenny. He thinks you're making a mistake.

Ray (*coming back*): Oh? Is that what the King of Mistakes thinks?

Josie: But he thinks she's pretty. How pretty?

Ray: Very. What's the word between divine and perfection?

Josie: Exaggeration. What's her name?

Ray: Sammii.

Josie: *Sammii*? With an I at the end?

Ray: Two I's.

Josie: Sammi-eye? . . . Has to be a model. How boring of you.

Ray: Right. It's really tedious waking up and seeing the face that graces eight magazine covers lying next to me.

Josie: You're *living* together?

Ray: I didn't say that. It's kind of loose. Not a commitment. I hope that word doesn't offend you.

Josie: I hear you can get about five good minutes of conversation out of her—a year.

Ray: Let me understand something. I didn't treat you very well last year and I'm not treating you very well *this* year. So what's your interest in me?

Josie: Next year. It'll give us time for our antipathy towards each other to cool off.

(*She touches him playfully. He backs up*)

Ray: Are—are you actually making a pass at me?

Josie: Oh, come on, Ray. We passed passes last year. We were mutually aggressive. Christ, it was like a car crash. But that was then. Now is different. Now, for some annoying reason . . . I'm suddenly nervous around you.

Ray: You? Nervous? Nah. Not your style.

Josie: And so are you. You're not even making eye contact.

Ray: Well, you keep batting your eyelashes so fast. I can't get a peek in.

Josie: You've come back to see me, haven't you? Twice today.

Ray: I didn't come back twice. I came back once. The first time I just came . . . to tell you off, and even if I *were* interested—

Josie (*moves closer*): Go slower. I like this part.

Ray: Well, it's not going to get better.

Josie: Sorry. I thought you said, "And even if I *were* interested."

Ray: I did. I can't . . . because Sammii's coming up on the bus in an hour.

Josie: *Today*? God, they're going to have to build another lane on the highway.

Ray: And even if she weren't—damn. I wish she weren't coming.

Josie: Do you. Ray? Really? Why?

Ray: I don't *know* why.

Josie: You seemed confused.

Ray: I know. I shouldn't have come back twice today.

Josie: You didn't come back twice. The first time you just . . .

Ray: I know! What do you think *confused* means? Look, I have to pick up Josie.

(*He starts to go*)

Josie: Sammii.

Ray: I *said* Sammii.

Josie: No, you said—

Ray: I said Josie but I was thinking Sammii. (*Looks around*) How do you get out of this place?

(*He goes quickly*)

Josie (*turns, just as Burt comes out of the house*): Did you get all that, Dad?

Burt: Yes. He said Josie but he was thinking Sammii.

(*She's gone into house. He notices Annie coming from behind the house, a cigarette in her hand*) I thought I heard you gave up smoking.

Annie: And I heard you've been sneaking in your share as well lately.

Burt: Well, some things stay in your blood, I guess—like some people.

Annie (*She looks at him, knowingly*): All these dead plants should have been pulled out, Burt. Who's been taking care of this place?

Burt: No one. Since you left, they won't let anyone touch them.

Annie: Is that why you called me in Paris? At midnight? For an emergency weed pulling? Christ, that call scared the hell out of me.

Burt: I didn't mean to. I needed to talk to you and I was afraid you might not come up this summer.

Annie: I only came because of Josie. I have other obligations now, Burt.

Burt: With Walter—yes? How is old Walt?

Annie: He's not old and he doesn't like to be called Walt.

Burt: Oh. Then don't tell him I said it. I'd hate to get into trouble with *young Wally*.

Annie: Your daughter just broke off an engagement and you don't seem the least bit phased by it.

Burt: I am extremely phased . . . But I'd feel worse if Josie married Kenny just to fulfill a commitment.

Annie: Well, it disturbed me. She seems to always rush headlong into things.

Burt (*nods*)**:** Yes. Like we did. We knew each other three weeks before we got married . . . Unfortunately we also rushed headlong *out* of things.

Annie: Nineteen years together is not exactly rushing. She never tells me anything. Is she alright?

Burt: Incredible. She's made this one of the best summers I ever had up here.

Annie: It's also one of the *only* summers you had up here.

Burt: True. But she's given me the chance to make up what I didn't give her for twenty-three years. My time.

Annie: And yet she's devoted to you. One of the blessings of being a father to a girl. Mothers aren't that lucky.

Burt: Come on, Annie, we both messed up. You got a divorce and I spent twenty-three years of weekends in a hot Buick on the New Jersey Turnpike. Too busy to know what I was missing.

Annie: As if you had to remind me.

Burt: No. I had to remind myself. It cost me a marriage.

Annie: Is that what it cost you, Burt? A marriage? It cost me half my life. And now half my family. There was no way to stop you. The minute you had one store, you had to open another. Why wasn't it enough, Burt? Two, three stores would have been plenty. We had enough money. Why was eight stores so important?

Burt: Because I was good at it. If Babe Ruth could hit sixty home runs, why should he stop at fifteen? The money never mattered to me. And what else was I going to do? I wasn't as smart as the kids are today. I had no special gifts. The only talent I had was to put in the time . . . and it wasn't just for me, Annie. It was for us.

Annie: For us? We would rather have had you than the time you put in. I never asked you for anything. Never wanted anything. (*Looks at the house*) Except this. This is what I wanted. It's not much but God I loved it. But as the years went by, I began to see the patterns. That waiting for you to come home was going to be our life. Whether here or in New York, you insisted I wait for you for dinner, while five, six nights a week, Josie ate by herself in the kitchen . . . And somewhere along the way, I lost her to Clemma.

Burt: Jesus, if it was so bad, Annie, why didn't you leave sooner?

Annie: Because I didn't have the courage. If I left you and took her too soon, knowing how much she loved you, I would have paid the price for it. So I stuck it out till she went to college—and I paid the price anyway.

Burt: Well, if nothing else, you got the marriage you deserved.

Annie: Really? Which marriage are you talking about?

Burt: Oh? I was under the impression you were happy now.

Annie: I am. Walter and I are good together. And he's always there for me. Always.

Burt: Is being good together the same as being in love?

Annie: No. Even when I left, I knew there'd be a part of me that would always love you. But as you get older, consistency and availability are more dependable . . . My mistake in life was not wanting another child. I thought you and Josie would be enough. (*She's lost in thought, then snaps out of it*) Am I depressing you as much as I'm depressing myself?

Burt: No. You just said you would always love me.

Annie: That's just a statement, Burt. Not an option. The truth is, it wouldn't have made any difference if I stayed or not. You were heading for that heart attack no matter what. And what I feared most, happened. That Josie would blame me for it.

Burt: We were divorced before the heart attack ever came.

Annie: Try telling her that.

Burt: I have. She knows. She'll work it through.

Annie: When? When will that be, Burt? Tell me.

Burt: Maybe this weekend. That's why I called you. Because if anything happens to me before you make your peace with her, it'll take that much longer.

Annie: *My* peace? Why is my crime bigger than yours? Why do I share more of the blame than you?

Burt: Because if something happens . . . if I die . . . I'm afraid that's what she'll remember.

Annie: What a terrible thing to say to me. What a terrible thing to put in anyone's mind.

Burt: I will do anything I can to help. Tell me what, Annie.

Annie: LIVE!! Live for another thirty years and *you* deal with her anger.

Burt: I hope I do, Annie.

Annie: Then try harder.

(*Clemma comes out*)

Clemma: Excuse me. Someone's here lookin' for Josie.

Burt: Who is it, Clemm?

Clemma: I think it's Mr. Miami. He may be wearin' a white suit but he don' look like no ice cream man to me.

Burt: Well, ask him in.

Clemma: You want him out here?

Burt: Please.

Clemma: I don' know why I'm askin' 'cause he's comin' anyway.

Annie: I'm asking God for help and he sends in Vinnie Bavasi.

(*Vinnie appears from center stage. Open-necked
dark sports shirt, a gold chain around his neck,
blue and white shoes, and white suit. He smiles a
lot, fixes his collar a lot. There's something very
cheery about him. His dialect is very New York*)

Vinnie: Hi! Vinnie Bavasi. Your lovely daughter's
friend from Miami.

Burt: Yes. and I'm—

Vinnie: Her father, right? (*Shakes Burt's hand vig-
orously*) A terrifically profound honor.

Burt: Oh. Yes. And this is—

Vinnie (*to Annie*): We met. Once again my pleasure. (*He shakes her hand, looks at her diamond ring, touches it, and smiles. Annie covers
her necklace with her hand*) Listen, can I use
your phone a minute? I think I just hit a deer down
the road.

Annie: Oh, my God.

Vinnie: Maybe it was a big dog because I don't think
deers bark. Anyway, he landed in the woods.
Maybe I could call a vet or someone.

Burt: Yes. Yes, of course.

Clemma: Phone's right in there.

Vinnie: Thanks. Nice seein' you, Mrs. Robbins (*He
gives her a quick scan*) Lookin' real good. (*He

Mel Winkler as Lewis Barnett and L. Scott Caldwell
as Clemma Diggins.
(All photographs of the Broadway production of Proposals by Carol Rosegg)

Kelly Bishop as Annie Robbins and Dick Latessa
as Burt Hines.

Suzanne Cryer as Josie Hines and Matt Letscher
as Ray Dolenz.

Katie Finneran as Sammii and Peter Rini
as Vinnie Bavasi.

smiles and winks. Not a pass, just friendly. He goes into house)

Clemma: Can't tell the difference between a dog and a deer? Glad *I* wasn't out there takin' a walk.

(*Josie hurries out of the house*)

Josie: Oh, God. He's really here. Who's he calling?

Burt: The vet.

Josie: Why?

Clemma: He hit a dog . . . or a deer.

Josie: With his car?

Annie: Maybe with his fist.

(*She shrugs, turns away*)

Josie: I *knew* I shouldn't have stayed for lunch.

(*She glares at Clemma. Kenny appears from off the path*)

Kenny: I decided to come. Oh, hello, Mrs. Robbins. Nice to see you.

Annie (*warmly*): Hello, Kenny dear . . . How's your mother?

Kenny: I don't know. She hasn't come out of her room all day . . . So, Josie, is your friend here? Because I'd really like to meet him.

Josie: No, you don't.

(*Vinnie comes out of the house*)

Vinnie: All set. They're gonna pick him up . . . Hey, Josie. You walk right by me? (*He picks her up in the air*) No hello, no smile, no nothin'. (*He puts her down*) This is one terrific girl you got here, Momma.

Annie (*aside to Burt*): He called me Momma.

Vinnie (*to Kenny*): Oh. Sorry. Din' notice you. (*puts his hand out*) Vinnie Bavasi. North Miami Beach, Florida.

Kenny (*doesn't shake his hand, crosses to Josie*): You break off our engagement yesterday and you invite a guy like this to lunch *today*?

Vinnie (*to Josie*): You broke off with this guy? (*He chuckles, looks at Kenny*) You gotta lotta nerve comin' to lunch? (*Kenny looks at him as if he's crazy, walks away from him. Vinnie looks around at the property, looks out front as if he's seeing it there as well*) Hey, this is nice—Very outdoorsy—I love the natural trees, know what I mean?

Clemma (*trying to save the day*): There's brandy in the house, if anyone wants.

(*Dim Out. Curtain.*)

ACT TWO

ACT II

Scene One

About an hour or so later.

A table has been put out for lunch with extra folding chairs brought out.

From the looks of the dishes, glasses, and remnants of food and drink, the meal is about over.

We sense an air of tension pervading the atmosphere. It must have been heavy going.

Seated around the table are Burt, Annie, Vinnie, Josie, and Kenny. Vinnie is at the middle of table, Kenny at the end.

Kenny: Alright, hold it. Wait a minute. Are you saying you shot him?

Vinnie: Yeah. I shot him. At the age of twelve, I shot a shark, big as a Cadillac with the trunk open. I was on Uncle Georgio's boat and he shoves a rifle in my hand and says, "You get one shot. Let's see how good you are, Spiff."

Kenny: Spiff?

Vinnie: Yeah. On accounta the spiffy suits I liked to wear.

Kenny: You wore spiffy suits when you were twelve?

Vinnie: Right. My Uncle Gino died and left me his suits. He was real short, you know, so they fit me . . . Anyway, the shark is bobbin' up and down, next to the boat, eight-foot-waves washin' over me. . . .

Kenny: The shark was next to the boat? Why didn't he swim away?

Vinnie: 'Cause Uncle Georgio had him on the line. One of those big cable jobs.

Kenny: A *cable?* You had him on a cable line and you *shot* him?

Vinnie: Oh. 'Scuse me. You don' consider this sport, I take it.

Kenny: Well, I admit there's more danger to it than killing them in *aquariums.*

Vinnie: Wit one bite, dis shark coulda eaten the back half of the boat, swallowin' Uncle Georgio, his wife Teresa, her sister Maria, and her three nephews . . . So when Uncle Georgio says to me, "Shoot!!" dis becomes a family affair.

Kenny: Did it ever occur to you that the shark had a family too?

Vinnie (*smiles, looks around, then to Kenny*): What are you, one of dose equalizationists?

Kenny: Equalizationists?

Vinnie: Yeah. Someone who thinks everything in the world is equal. Well, it ain't. Someone always got the avantage.

Kenny: The *avant*age?

Vinnie: Yeah. Like in this conversation right now, between you and me, who do you think has the avantage?

Kenny: You do. You have the *avant*age.

Vinnie: And why is dat?

Kenny: Because you're speaking a language I don't understand.

Vinnie (*points finger at him*): *Right!* Same thing with me and the shark. Because no matter how I try, I don' speak shark.

(*The others all look at each other*)

Kenny: And what does the shark speak?

Vinnie: He speaks nine hunnert pounds and a mouthful of cutlery.

Kenny: Cutlery?

Vinnie: Knives. A mouthful of sharp knives. I'm usin' a different word to paint a picture here.

Burt: Yes. It's a metaphor.

Vinnie (*to Burt*): No. It's cutlery.

Josie: I think we all get what you're saying, Vinnie.

Vinnie: Okay. So he got the avantage 'cause all I got is a rifle. One rifle, one bullet. And I'm only a twelve-year-old kid.

Kenny: Wearing your Uncle Gino's suit.

Vinnie (*stares at him*): What's dat got to do with it?

Kenny: Well, a twelve-year-old kid in a man's suit might confuse the shark . . . giving *you* the *avant*age.

(*There is a silence. They all look at Vinnie, waiting for his answer*)

Vinnie: No! He don't know nothin' about men's apparel. He knows about a rifle 'cause he's seen one before.

Kenny: Like every time your family goes fishing?

Vinnie: Right. In the first place, it's more humaneable.

Kenny: *Humane-able?*

Josie: Let it go, Kenny.

Vinnie: Look, if you don't shoot him, you gotta drag him through the water for six, ten hours from Miami to Fort Lauderdale . . . So I take my one shot and *pow*, the next thing he knows, he's lyin' on a plate next to a baked potato, sour cream, and chives.

(*Josie looks away disgustedly*)

Kenny (*turns to Josie*): And what do *you* think about all this, Josie?

Josie: I don't know. I'm a vegetarian.

(*She walks away*)

Kenny: Well, maybe Vinnie'll shoot some vegetables for you.

Annie (*stands*): Anyone want to help with the dishes?

Kenny: Sure. Throw them up in the air for Vinnie.

(*He mimes shooting a rifle in the air*)

Josie: Stop it, Kenny.

Vinnie: It would give me great pleasure to wash dem dishes. If I may just have a smoke first. (*He takes out a long cigar*) Mr. Hines? Care for a pure Habana?

Burt: *Habana?*

Vinnie: Yeah. I'm sayin' it the Cuban way. It means— Havana.

Burt: Oh. Like avantage?

Vinnie: No. Avantage is English.

Kenny: Wanna bet?

(*Josie throws her arms in the air*)

Kenny: Well, Vinnie, you certainly have some interesting thoughts about death and valor and dying and death . . . I guess we just come from different schools of thought.

Vinnie (*lighting his cigar*): True. Only my school ain't Harvard, in case you was wondering.

Kenny: You can't imagine the disappointment up in Cambridge.

Josie: Is anyone going to stop them?

Vinnie (*smiles*): No, no. It's okay, Josie. (*Smiles*) You see, Kenny thinks 'cause I dress a little colorfully, and I talk a little picturesque-wally, that I'm what? (*Looks at Kenny*) Ignorant? Is dat what you think, Kenny?

Kenny: Not at all. I think of you as being very . . . unique-wally.

Vinnie (*he stands*): Okay. There's no such word as unique-wally. And I know when I say right words and wrong words. And sometimes I pick the wrong word knowledgeingly . . . Like that one . . . Because everyone here will remember it. And maybe they'll tell people what dis guy, Vinnie Bavasi, said at lunch . . . It's what you call style. And I believe style should be in the way you dress, in the way you talk, and in the way you live. And I live . . . style-ishously.

(*He lights cigar*)

Burt: Well, I think we'd all agree with that, Kenny.

Vinnie: And as it happens, Ken, yours truly *did* go to college.

Annie: You *did??* I'm sorry. That came out wrong . . . Where did you go, Vinnie?

Vinnie: Well, no one here would have heard of it.

Kenny: We all know that, but tell us anyway.

Vinnie: It's a small school near Pensacola, Florida— Chockpaw Community College.

Kenny (*to Vinnie*): Really? And who founded Chockpaw?

Vinnie: I found it, in Pensacola.

Kenny: So what kind of school is it? Arts? Science? Flamingo Hunting? Something like that?

Burt: Josie, would you see if Clemma has any more of those tuna cookies?

Josie: Not *everything* was tuna fish, Dad.

Vinnie: Be that as it may, I thought that tuna was of superiority quality.

Kenny (*jumps up*): Jesus! How can you people sit here and listen to this vaudeville act? This guy is pulling our legs.

Vinnie (*points a finger at Kenny*): Okay, Kenny. These people were nice enough to feed your mouth, now shut it up.

Burt (*stands quickly*): Alright, boys. Tug-of-war is over. Vinnie, you like baseball? We get the Yankee games up here. Should be on now.

Vinnie: Invitation accepted . . . If the ladies will excuse me?

Annie: Oh, yes. We'll clean up. Josie and I can do it in a jiffaly . . . jiffy . . . You two go on.

Vinnie: As you wish. (*He gets up*) Oh, er, Josie. We gonna have a chance to talk in private later? You and me?

Josie: Oh. Er, talk? . . . Well, sure. Why not?

Vinnie: 'Cause I got some personal things to discuss. Anywhere's you want. I trust you.

(*He smiles and winks at Kenny, shoots him with his finger, and goes into the house followed by Burt*)

Kenny (*to Josie*): Why not go for a ride with him in his *slaughter-mobile*? He already hit a deer, maybe he'll get Bambi's *father* this time.

Josie: I'm hoping he'll tell me what he has to say and leave. I'm being polite. You're the one who's agitating him.

Annie (*lowers her voice*): Will everyone please calm down. And Josie's right, Kenny. You *were* pushing things too far. (*To Josie. She starts to go with dishes*) Josie, I think you and I ought to have ourselves a little talk later.

(*She goes into kitchen door*)

Kenny: Everyone gets a time slot with you today. Got any openings about two in the morning?

Josie: Kenny, we've just been through a lot. Only the Last Supper could be more emotional than that lunch. I'm exhausted.

Kenny: Look, if you tell me he doesn't mean anything to you, then I'll accept it.

Josie: He doesn't mean anything to me.

Kenny: Then why is he here?

Josie: I *told* you. I didn't invite him. I didn't tell him to come.

Kenny: Then why don't you tell him to leave?

Josie: Why don't *you* tell him?

Kenny: Can I? Please. I'd *love* the *avant*age of telling him to go.

(*He starts for the house*)

Josie: KENNY!! (*He stops. She lowers her voice*) Listen. There are other people here today. Many of them with their own problems. Can we stop thinking of ourselves for five minutes? Please?

Kenny: I'm sorry. You're right. And it's not jealousy, I swear, I understand our breakup. I'm just not creative enough for you. Not artistic enough. I wish I could paint. I wish I could sculpt. I wish I could write. That's why I envy Ray.

Josie: Ray??

Kenny: See, that's the kind of person you need.

Josie: You think I need Ray?

Kenny: *No!* Not literally. But I mean someone with his sensibilities.

Josie: Why do you diminish yourself so much, Kenny? You have every bit as much sensibility as Ray does.

Kenny: I do? Okay. Then how about me? (*She turns away*) It was a joke. I made a joke about myself, Josie. A small step towards flamboyancy . . . So who knows how much I'll change from now on.

Josie: Kenny, *PLEASE!!* . . . I have to talk to Vinnie. I have to talk to my mother. I have to calm Clemma down. I have to call the vet to see if the animal Vinnie hit needs blood or something. I JUST DON'T WANT TO TALK ANYMORE, ALRIGHT?

(*She rushes into the house, slamming the door. Kenny stands there, furious with himself*)

Kenny: You IDIOT!! Will you *shut up*, Kenny? Shut your jealous, paranoidal, self-indulgent, self-destructive MOUTH!

(*Furiously, he picks up a medium-sized rock and heaves it into the bushes. From the bushes we hear a girl scream out, then a man's voice calls out*)

Man: Hey! Are you crazy? What the hell's wrong with you? (*It's Ray. He rushes out, sees Kenny*) Was that *you?* You looking to kill somebody?

Kenny: I'm sorry. I didn't know anyone was there. Did I hit you?

Ray: No, but you almost took Sammii's head off.

(*Sammii comes out of the woods. She's about twenty-three and gorgeous, in a model sort of way. She is extremely upset, and not terribly bright*)

Sammii (*near tears*): Oh, Ray. It was just awful.

Kenny: I'm sorry. I'm really sorry.

Ray: It didn't hit you, did it?

Sammii: No. But it killed a bird . . . His poor little head is smashed in like a melon.

Kenny: Oh, great.

Ray: He didn't mean it.

Sammii: A beautiful little blue bird with a yellow breast . . . Why were you throwing at birds?

Kenny: I wasn't throwing at birds. I was throwing at the world. The bird just happened to be living in the world I threw it in.

Sammii: There's nothing *out* there but birds. You'd have to be blind to miss one.

Kenny: Why does my life keep getting worse?

Ray (*looks around*): Where is everyone?

Kenny: The ladies are in the house. Josie's dad is watching baseball with this fish murderer named Vinnie Bavasi.

Sammii: Shouldn't we bury it or something?

Kenny: I will. I promise. I'll attend to all the funeral arrangements. This Vinnie guy got me crazy.

Sammii: The poor thing never had a chance. He was sitting on this branch whistling. Maybe to his little chicks.

Kenny: I didn't single him out. I had no grudge against this bird. (*To Ray*) I hated this guy.

Ray: You mean she just invited him here?

Kenny: No. He drove up on his own. Knocked a dog off his fender and into the vet's operating room.

Sammii: Oh, my God!! What's *wrong* with you people up here??

Ray: It was really an accident.

Kenny: This idiot says words like pictur-esqually . . . He went to school at *Chockpaw.* Their English Department was the entire Al Capone gang.

Sammii: Chockpaw? What's wrong with Chockpaw? Buzzi Bando, my best friend in the world, went there. I hear it's a really good school.

Kenny: Yes, I know. I just met the man who founded it (*To Ray*) The day after she broke our engagement.

Ray (*to Kenny*): Well, he doesn't sound like her type.

Kenny: I was *engaged* to her and I wasn't her type . . . Actually, *you're* her type.

Ray: She said that?

Kenny: No, I did.

Sammii: *You* did? You're trying to fix my guy up with a girl you were engaged to? Why don't you throw rocks at *her* instead of innocent birds?

Kenny (*to Sammii*): How do you know he was innocent? Maybe every bird in the forest hated him . . . Maybe I did this region a big favor.

(*This is all getting to him now*)

Sammii: You are just overly weird, Kenny.

Kenny: Well, then you and Josie should get along just fine.

(*Josie comes out of the house*)

Josie: Who should get along just fine with Josie? (*Sees Ray*) Oh. Hi, Ray.

Ray (*to Josie*): Josie, this is my friend, Sammii. Sammii, this is Josie.

Josie: Hello.

Sammii: Hi . . . Ray, I'd like to go back to the room. I can still see that bird back there with his brains bashed in.

Josie: Oooh. What bird?

Sammii: He's back there. Hit with a rock.

Josie: Who would do a thing like that? (*Kenny turns his head away. Ray looks down*) Was it Vinnie?

Kenny: Yes.

Ray: *YES???*

Kenny: In a way. He got me so goddamn mad. I picked up a rock and heaved it.

Josie: At a bird?

Kenny: It was an accident. I haven't been sitting up, planning this for months.

Josie: Are you sure he's dead?

Sammii: Well, his head's *stuck* to the tree so I would think so.

Josie: Let's take a look. Sometimes birds have incredible recovery powers.

Sammii: He won't recover unless you give this bird a whole new head . . . I'll show you where he is.

(*She starts to move*)

Kenny (*following Sammii*): I'll make it up to you. I'll buy a new bird for the forest.

Sammii (*amazed at him*): You think the other birds won't know the difference? God!

(*She is gone, with Kenny right behind her*)

Josie: So that's Sammii. Somehow I had a different picture of her.

Clemma: *Josie!!* Your mother wants to see you.

Josie: I'll be right back. I'm going to a funeral.

(*She goes off*)

Clemma: In the woods? Who died?

Ray: A bird. No one you know.

(*Ray goes off*)

Clemma: A bird, heh? (*She sits on the porch steps, looks out at the audience*) What'd I tell you? They die droppin' outta the skies 'round here, but I never see 'em. Did you? Well, we got through the lunch alright, but I'll tell you the truth. I couldn't keep up with all the criss-crossin' between who wanted who, who wanted out, who wanted in, who was gonna get and who was gonna be forgot . . . Now, I may not be tellin' it straight because as I said, this all happened 'bout fifty years ago, three of which I been dead . . . but one thing I still remember. I felt somethin' brewin' in the air that day . . . somethin' like a storm comin' up . . . not the kinda storm that blows and roars down from heaven. This was the kinda thunder that only people with discontent and achin' hearts could make . . .

(*She gets up. She starts folding a tablecloth. As she does, we see an African-American man, early fifties, slight graying in the hair, carrying one old suitcase, appear. Her back is to him. He moves down a little closer, then stops. She never turns, then says—*)

Clemma: How long you been standin' there, Lewis?

Lewis: Seems like six years.

Clemma: Seven.

Lewis: I never was good at sneakin' up on you.

Clemma: Not as good as sneakin' out. (*She turns, looks at him*) Don' you *dare* tell me I got older.

Lewis: No need to say what I don' see . . . You look just fine to me, sugar.

Clemma: *Sugar??* Don' you sugar me, Lewis. You left all the sugar in the bowl when you walked out.

Lewis: I suppose you're right.

Clemma: You don' have to suppose. I said it so I'm right. You get shorter or something'?

Lewis: Just bent a little. All them years of givin' haircuts to kids gonna unstraighten a man's back . . . I mean it sincerely when I say you're lookin' real fine, Clemma.

Clemma: I can look better than this. But I wasn't gonna dress up and give you this meetin' any more importance than it deserved . . . You just passin' through these parts?

Lewis: Well, I might pass through . . . I was hopin' I might not.

Clemma: Hmmm . . . You hungry?

Lewis: For your cookin'? Always.

Clemma: I got some pecan pie left over that Josie made me put aside for you. I was gonna throw it out.

Lewis: May I sit a minute? (*She shrugs. He sits. He looks tired*) I ain't seen Josie since she was this high . . . You still runnin' this family, Clem?

Clemma: Ain't much family left to run. Mrs. Hines got divorced. She's Mrs. Robbins now. And Mr. Hines ain't hardly Mr. Hines no more. Gave up his business after one heart attack too many.

Lewis: Oh. I'm sorry. I didn't know.

Clemma: 'Course you didn't know. They don' have no mailman knows where *you* live.

Lewis (*nods*): I tried callin' you a few times.

Clemma: How hard you try? 'Cause I never got no messages.

Lewis: I didn't say I called. I tried to. Just couldn't find the nerve . . . I didn't think you'd want to hear anything I had to say.

Clemma: No. I didn't. What makes you think I want to hear it now?

Lewis: 'Cause when I called, you didn' say nothing 'bout bein' with someone else.

Clemma: Ha. You men are funny. You think I've been twiddlin' my thumbs for seven years waitin' for you to come back? I have made my share of friends, Lewis. I did not twiddle my thumbs alone. But I didn' attach to anyone 'cause I never met a man more dependable than you, which tells you what a low opinion I got of men.

Lewis: You don't look older, Clem, but you sure put on a hard edge.

Clemma: I didn't put it on. You left it with me. Why you keep lookin' at me outta the side of your head? You got the arthritis, Lewis?

Lewis: No. Just can't see outta this eye. Went blind in there 'bout four years ago.

Clemma: Is that the truth? I'm sorry. I never wished you no harm, Lewis.

Lewis: Wasn't your fault. Doctor said it was a cataract.

Clemma: I was wonderin' why you didn' think I looked any older (*she stops a second*) I *did* wish bad things on you, Lewis. But I never said them loud enough for the Lord to hear. Well, you just sit there and look at what you can see of the scenery and I'll get you some of that pie.

(*She goes in the kitchen door. Vinnie comes out from the porch door. He looks around and sees Lewis*)

Vinnie: Hi. Vinnie Bavasi.

Lewis: Oh. Hello. Lewis Barnett.

(*Vinnie puts hand out. They shake*)

Vinnie: You work here, Lewis, or was you invited to this tuna luncheon?

Lewis (*laughs*): Me? No. I'm just here to see Clemma.

Vinnie: I got your meanin'. I'm here to see Josie. Have you seen her?

Lewis: Oh, not since she was a teenager.

Vinnie (*thinks, then*): No, I'm not goin' that far back. I mean *today*. I'm lookin' for her.

Clemma (*calls out from kitchen*): She's in the woods attendin' a bird funeral. Over that way.

Vinnie: Hey, thanks, Clem. (*To Lewis*) Enjoyed makin' the contact, Lew. See ya. (*To Clemma*) And lemme say, your tuna fish was eminently tasteable. (*He winks at Lewis and goes*)

Lewis (*to himself*): Tasteable?

(*Clemma comes out with a piece of pie and a cup of coffee*)

Clemma: I put some cream on it for you.

Lewis: Maybe I shouldn't eat this until you hear what I have to say.

Clemma (*she stops*): You should have told me before I put the cream on it. (*She puts it on the table, then backs off*) But alright, go on. I'll listen.

Lewis: Well, Clemma, I'll be the first one to say I have not lived a righteous life.

Clemma: No you'd be the second one 'cause I was the *first* one to say it.

Lewis: If you're gonna listen, woman, then listen . . . I have always been a man who had to be on the move. Couldn't get the Navy life outta my system . . . I lived with a woman in Chicago and never told her I was married. And I had a child with another woman in St. Louis who didn't care if I was married or not. I supported the child until I lost my job and then I lost the woman when I lost my eye . . . Sometimes them losses just keep pilin' up. (*He looks at her. She just stares at him*) I guess you don' wanna hear about Pittsburgh.

Clemma: I wish I didn't hear *any* of that. 'Cause it just proves what a cold and heartless woman I am . . . because I have no compassion for your pain or your losses or your sightlessness . . . I was brought up in church not to be a vengeful woman, but by God, if I was you, I'd do everything in my power to protect that other eye. . . .

(*She turns away*)

Lewis: I can't undo the things I did that was wrong.

Clemma: Uh huh.

Lewis: And I can't give back the years that was lost to you.

Clemma: Uh huh.

Lewis: And I wouldn't blame you if you chased me outta this chair and outta your sight right now.

Clemma: Uh huh.

Lewis: Damn it, Clemma, I can't apologize if you're gonna "uh huh" everything I got to say.

Clemma: I don' hear no apologizin'. All I hear is what you can't help, can't fix, or can't give back to me . . . What you comin' 'round here for anyway? You don' need me and I don' need you . . . You won't have no trouble findin' yourself another woman. Just keep your blind eye closed, they'll think you're winkin' at 'em.

Lewis: Clemma . . . You are the *only* woman that I want.

Clemma: Since when? What's so special about me, Lewis, that you have to see once every seven years?

Lewis: Meanin' why did I up and leave in the first place? . . . Well, lately I've been thinkin' about that.

Clemma: If it just come up *lately*, I ain't interested.

Lewis: Will you let me *talk*, Clemma? You *always* had to have the last word, didn't you? A man doesn't like to hear that. I never did.

Clemma: Alright . . . Go on . . . Say what's on your mind. (*She sits opposite him*)

Lewis: I knew what it meant to you to be without a child. And when the doctor told you you'd never be able to have your own, I thought it was my fault. I thought that time we had that scuffle on the stairs when you found out some bad things, that I killed every baby you could ever have. But you looked at the doctor and said, "Well, I still got my Lewis so God must still love me anyways." (*He looks at her. Her eyes move away at the memory of that moment*) I have never felt guilt like that, in all my life. And it was that guilt that drove me away, Clemma. Because I had no call gettin' so much love from such a good woman.

Clemma: That's right. You didn't. But there was somethin' I never told you . . . I knew I could never have a child long before I fell down those stairs. Long before I met you. And I didn't tell you 'bout it after the accident, 'cause I thought your guilt would keep you from ever leaving me . . . Well, we was both wrong, wasn't we?

Lewis: Yes . . . If you kept that from me for so long, why you telling it to me now?

Clemma: Because it was time to unload something that was sittin' heavy on my conscience. Just 'cause you was a sinner, Lewis, didn't mean I was a saint.

Lewis: You don't have to be so harsh on yourself, Clemma.

Clemma: Yes, I do, 'cause I ain't through accusin' you yet. The truth is, it wasn't your guilt that drove you away. You just had a roving eye for other women . . . And the Lord fixed that, didn't he?

Lewis: I guess he did.

Clemma (*shakes her head*): What a pair of fools and liars we were, Lewis.

Lewis: Ain't that the truth?

Clemma: But maybe it was all God's plan. Maybe I was meant to lose you and find someone like Josie to fill my life.

Lewis: Well, if it was God's plan, maybe He ain't finished yet.

Clemma: Meanin' what?

Lewis: Well, Josie may be ready to move on with her own life. So maybe the plan was for me to re-enter the picture now.

Clemma: You lookin' for me to take care of you? I ain't the Lord's unemployment office, you know.

Lewis: I'll find work. I always have.

Clemma: Cuttin' hair?

Lewis: No. I gave up cuttin' hair because of this. (*He holds up his left hand. The fingers are gnarled and almost closed*) Woke up one mornin' and the fingers went dead on me. Can't hold a scissors in it and tha's the one I had my talent in. I'm just learnin' to tie my shoes with one hand.

Clemma: Lewis, you are somethin', ain't you? If you got any more things that have gone dead or ain't workin', tell me now and get it over with.

Lewis: No. Tha's it. Except for my blind eye and dead fingers, I'm healthy as a horse.

Clemma: A horse like that would have trouble findin' work too. (*She moves away from the table*) No. It's too late, Lewis. Too late for me to ever get hurt like that again.

Lewis: It wouldn't happen again, Clemma. I'm a changed man.

Clemma (*nods*): I can see that from here, Lewis.

Lewis: Well, you think about it. I have a friend I can stay with. Has a gas station up the road a few miles.

Clemma: I'd a felt more wanted than needed if you'd come back here before all hell broke loose in your body.

Lewis: I can still see what I want and I got the strength in my good hand to take care of both of us. You ponder it, Clemma. That's all I ask.

(*Disappointed, he gets up, puts on his hat, picks up his bag, turns to go*)

Clemma: You didn't eat your pie.

Lewis: I'll take it with me, if you don't mind.

(*He starts to put a napkin over it*)

Clemma (*she watches him, then—*): Lewis! I got a lotta extra work to do today. I guess I could use another hand around here.

Lewis (*smiles, holds up right hand*): You mean like this one?

(*She covers her face and laughs*)

Clemma: Excuse me for laughin'.

Lewis: That's more than I was hopin' for.

Clemma: You can stay till after dinner, if you want.

Lewis: That's more than I was expectin'.

Clemma: I'll tell you this, Lewis. I'm puzzled. 'Cause I don' know who the Lord's lookin' after now. You . . . or me.

(*Their eyes meet. Music between change*)

ACT II

Scene Two

Josie, Kenny, Sammii, Vinnie and Ray are standing in a semi-circle. Sammii, in the center, is holding an open shoe box in which lies the dead bird. They are solemn. Their heads are bowed.

Sammii: We lay to rest this small creature from God's . . . from God's . . . (*She looks for help*)

Ray: Feathered Kingdom?

Sammii: . . . from God's feathered Kingdom . . . whose innocent beauty returns from . . . from . . . (*She looks at Ray again*)

Ray: . . . whence it came.

Sammii: Whence it came . . . taken too soon from those who loved him.

Kenny (*aside*): *Loved* him? You never even met him.

Ray: Knock it off, Kenny.

Kenny (*to God*): Forgive me.

Sammii: What do we do now?

Vinnie: Well, let's toss some dirt and a few twigs in with the little guy.

Kenny (*to Vinnie*): Is that what you usually do, Vinnie?

(*Vinnie wants to move at him but he's restrained*)

Josie: Vinnie's right. Everyone get some dirt and twigs.

(*All except Sammii get down, looking for dirt and twigs*)

Sammii: Is this the only shoe box you have?

Josie: What's wrong with it?

Sammii: Well, it says Florsheim Shoes on it. Is that appropriate?

Kenny: I don't think anyone makes funeral shoe boxes for birds, Sammii.

(*They all glare at him*)

Josie: Sammii, you pick a spot and we'll bury him.

Sammii: There was a hill back there . . . with a wonderful view.

Kenny: That's good, He'll like that. (*They all glare at him again*) Why was that wrong?

Josie: Can we just go, please.

(*They all turn to go except Vinnie*)

Vinnie: Not yet.

(*Vinnie's head is down, as if in prayer. They look at him wondering. He lifts his head and starts to sing "Amazing Grace." On the third line, Sammii crosses to him and sings along. They all look at each other, then cross and join them, singing as well. Kenny hasn't moved. Just before the last line, they stop and look at Kenny. Embarrassed, he crosses to them and they all finish the song together*)

(*Music under change.*)

ACT II

Scene Three

Lewis is unfolding the table quickly as we hear a clap of thunder. Clemma is rushing to the house with the pie dish and the coffee cup. The following dialogue ensues as they rush back and forth, putting the chairs and table onto the porch.

Clemma: Hurry up, Lewis, 'fore we get a downpour.

Lewis: Looks to me like it's blowin' the other way.

Clemma: Well, right now I ain't countin' on *how* things look to you.

(*Lewis laughs*)

Clemma: What you laughin' at, Lewis?

Lewis: I don't know. I'm feelin' kinda good. Can't remember when the last time I had a good laugh was.

Clemma: Well, you didn't tell me about Pittsburgh so it musta been then.

Lewis: Now take a look at me, Clemma. I may have a handicap or two, but this young man is movin' real fast.

Clemma: Yes, you are. 'Cause you been practicin' for the past seven years.

(*All the furniture is in by now. So are Lewis and Clemma. Vinnie and Sammii appear on the path. The thunder has all but stopped*)

Vinnie: Well, you probably never heard of it. Little school called Chockpaw Community College.

Sammii: I know Chockpaw. I had a friend who went there. Maybe you know her. Buzzi Bando.

Vinnie: Buzzi Bando? Yeah, I knew her. I knew her pretty good. I was engaged to her, that's how good I knew her.

Sammi: Engaged?

Vinnie: Oh, yeah. We was headin' as they say, altarwise, until Buzzi decided *other*wise. Said she wanted to go to New York and try this modeling thing.

Sammii: Well, she didn't have to try very hard because she's been on the cover of every magazine you can mention. Did you know that?

Vinnie: Sure. She sends 'em to me. If you ask me, they over make her up too much.

Sammii: Did you ever try to get in touch with her?

Vinnie: Yeah. I sent back her magazines. Took a black marker and scrawled "Who cares?" on her face.

Sammii: Wow! I bet that hurt her.

Vinnie: No. It was just on the magazines . . . So I hear you're a model too.

Sammii: Me? Well, just beginning. I'm not in Buzzi's class.

Vinnie: Why not? She's no prettier than you.

Sammii: Oh. Thanks. But it's not about being pretty. It's about whether the camera likes you or not.

Vinnie: I'd break the camera that didn't like you.

Sammi (*smiles*)**:** No one ever said *that* to me before.

Vinnie: Well, it's an unusual sentence.

Sammii: So what do you do?

Vinnie: I work part time for my Uncle Georgio. Biggest foreign car distributor in South Florida.

Sammii: And what do you do the other part time?

Vinnie (*he looks around*)**:** You promise you won't laugh?

Sammii: Cross my heart . . . What do you do?

Vinnie: I make my own jewelry—not for sale. Just for friends, family. Sounds a little fruity, right?

Sammi: No. I don't think that's fruity at all. What have you made?

Vinnie (*fingers chain on his neck*): This gold chain. You notice the intricate detail? The links are intraceptable to the naked eye . . . Look close.

Sammi (*leans in and looks*): You're right. I can hardly see them.

Vinnie: You like this ring? A genuine Bavasi.

Sammii: Incredible. Did you make the diamond too?

Vinnie: No, you can't make diamonds, you get 'em from a wholesaler . . . How about this watch? Swiss movement.

Sammi (*taking no notice*): You made *that?*

Vinnie: Just the outside. I need a Swiss guy for the movement.

(*She looks at him in amazement. He leans over and kisses her mouth, then backs away*)

Sammii: So, what made you get interested in this?

Vinnie: Well, when I was a kid, we went to see my family in Italy. And one day we go to the Vatican. The place where the Pope lives.

Sammii: Yes. I know.

Vinnie: And in these glass cases, I see all these silver and gold crosses and these diamond entrusted sceptricals . . . Is that right?

Sammii: Sceptricals? I'm not sure.

Vinnie: Kings hold 'em in their arms to let people know they're Kings.

Sammii: Skeptres, I think.

Vinnie: Oh. Skeptres. Right . . . Anyway, I get this catalogue, "Treasures of the Vatican" . . . and I see these pictures of the world's greatest treasures, works of unimaginable valuable-ness, and I say to myself, "Hey! I can do that." But what I wanna do, is make somethin' good enough to give to the Pope . . . from the People of South Florida.

Sammii: You are so special.

Vinnie: Now I know I'm not good enough yet. And I know if I make, what? Like a gold I.D. bracelet, the Pope ain't gonna wear it. 'Cause if he lost it, people already *know* where he lives, right?

Sammii (*amused*): Do they ever.

Vinnie: So I make all this stuff for practice. But one day, before I die, I'm gonna get a handwritten note from the Pope that says, "Dear Vinnie, Adomino, Adominus, and thank you, People of South Florida" . . . Crazy, heh?

Sammii: No, not at all. So where do you know Josie from?

Vinnie: Met her in Miami. Danced with her once. Took her for a walk. This is one smart girl, this Josie. She stopped me from doin' somethin' real stupid once.

Sammii: What was that?

Vinnie: Well, I started tellin' her about Buzzi dumping me. And I tell Josie my plan, which is this . . . I was gonna fly up to New York, kidnap Buzzi, bring her back to Florida, and lock her in my basement until she says yes.

Sammii: You're joking?

Vinnie: No. So Josie turns to me and gives me one word of advice . . . One little word . . . She says, "Don't!" . . . I hardly knew the girl and she says to me, "Don't!" . . . and I didn't. Because I trusted her.

Sammii: That is an incredible story.

Vinnie: Now I just gotta get her alone for two minutes, 'cause I got this little present I made for her.

Sammii: May I ask what?

Vinnie: A brewch. A solid gold brewch . . . that says, "Don't." You think she'll like it?

Sammii: What girl wouldn't?

Vinnie: You know you're easier to talk to than Buzzi. You involved with anyone?

Sammii: Well, sort of. With Ray . . . I think he really wants to get serious . . . But I'm just not ready to get involved . . . especially with a writer . . . because they're thinkin' all the time . . . I like that you talk and that you never think.

Vinnie: Thank you.

Sammi: I'm looking to break it off but I just don't know how to tell him without hurting him.

Vinnie: That's no problem. *I'll* tell him.

Sammii: Oh, no.

Vinnie (*gets up, energized*): Sure. It's more humane. Don't dangle a guy on a rod and reel. Cut the line or shoot him. I know. Come on.

(*He pulls her off into the woods. We hear thunder. Annie comes out and looks up at the sky*)

Annie: Well, I had my car washed, so naturally it's going to pour.

(*Burt comes out*)

Annie: Where do you think the kids are? I hope they have enough sense to come out of the rain. (*Burt is smiling at her. She looks at him*) What are you smiling at?

Burt: I just remembered what you and I used to do up here on rainy afternoons.

Annie: Oh, Burt. Behave yourself. Go inside. I'll wait till the kids come back.

Burt: Josie'll take care of them . . . I swear, you don't look much older than when we first got married.

Annie: Well, squint and you'll see the difference.

(*She looks out for kids*)

Burt (*looks up from the porch*): I bet we get at least an hour of rain . . . An hour's a long time, Annie.

Annie: Burt, please. There's a lot of tension going on up here.

Burt: I know. That's why it's thundering. Helps release the tension. Don't look away.

Annie: Burt, don't do this.

Burt: I'm not doing anything. At least not without your help. (*He extends his hand*) Will you just take my hand?

Annie: Take your pills. This is ridiculous.

Burt: Why?

Annie: Why? Because you're ill and I'm married.

Burt: Right. And you came all the way from Paris to see me.

Annie: Because I sensed how ill you are. I came to see you, Burt, not to kill you . . . Oh, God, forgive me for saying that, Burt.

Burt: I forgive you everything . . . I love you, Annie. I always have, always will.

Annie (*looks at him*): Burt, don't—

Burt: Just hear me out. (*The telephone rings. He pays no attention*) When you first left, I was sure you'd be back. Then, when I knew it was over, I was angrier than I ever thought I could be . . . then came a sense of loss . . . followed by a deep, dark despair . . . I had no choice but to learn to live with it. But then something happened . . . this summer. Up here . . . I started to realize I was robbing myself of something very precious . . . the memories . . . Of all that was good. I was blocking them out, giving them up, tossing them away . . . and I missed them . . . I forgot that if I allowed myself, I could keep them forever . . . The twenty-one years we were married . . . and the two years before . . . when you worked all week and spent your weekends helping me open the first store. And the thing that became so clear to me, was that loving you was only a part of it. The other part, was how much I enjoyed you. I *liked* you as much as I loved you, Annie . . . and I don't think I ever told you that.

Annie: Oh, God, Burt, if this is a goodbye speech, I couldn't bear it.

Burt: No, I'm not ready for anything like that yet . . . But you owe me something, Annie.

Annie: What?

Burt: I'm asking you to stand right there . . . to give me the opportunity to tell you . . . that I think you're perfectly swell.

(*She is touched more than she can imagine*)

Annie: Oh, God, Burt . . .

(*He moves towards her just as Clemma comes out of the kitchen door*)

Clemma: Oh. Excuse me. Mrs. Robbins, you got a person to person call from Paris, France. (*She looks at Burt, sensing what's going on*) I could tell him to call back, if you want.

Burt: Take the call . . . it's fine.

(*Annie turns and goes into the house*)

Clemma: Mr. Hines . . . I'm so sorry.

(*She turns to go in. Burt just stands there. Josie enters*)

Josie: What's Clemma sorry about?

Burt: Telephone calls.

(*He exits into the woods. Ray enters*)

Ray: Oh. There you are . . . Where'd you disappear to?

Josie: Nowhere. Why? Were you looking for me?

Ray: Well, Kenny left after the second chorus of Amazing Grace . . . Vinnie wandered off with Sammii talking about an afterlife because he's a reincarnationalist . . . and suddenly you left and I was alone.

Josie: I wasn't sure you wanted to see me.

Ray: No, actually I *did* want to see you. I thought I owed you an apology.

Josie: For what?

Ray: For coming down on you so hard . . . I was angry for Kenny's sake but it wasn't my place to tell you off.

Josie: No, Ray. You don't owe me an apology.

Ray: Well, keep it anyway. It's always nice to have an extra apology around. Anyway, I'll be leaving in a few days.

Josie: Where are you going?

Ray (*takes letter from out of his back pocket*)**:** I found this letter under my door. It's from Random House.

Josie: Good news, I hope.

Ray: Partly, I don't have to return their meager advance. They dropped the option on my book.

Josie: Oh, Ray. I'm so sorry.

Ray: It's okay. I got a better offer. Assistant golf pro in Houston. It's good money and they don't expect rewrites.

Josie: What's the rush to get to Houston? Send the book somewhere else.

Ray: This *was* somewhere else. Scribners and Doubleday already rejected it. (*He looks at the letter*) I want to keep this. If nothing else, I finally got my name on something put out by Random House.

Josie: There's something else going on here. Something you're not telling me. You didn't walk away from me last summer just because of Kenny, did you? What was it, Ray?

Ray: I got scared.

Josie: Of me?

Ray: No. Of me. Because I felt such a pressure from you, such an overblown belief in such a modest talent. That if I ever tried to reach as high as your expectations, they'd pick up the pieces of my ego with a tweezer.

Josie: I didn't know I was doing that to you.

Ray: It's not what you do, Josie. It's what you are. It's what you expect without ever asking for it.

Josie: What do you think I expect? Success?

Ray: Worse. You want quality. Patience. Stamina. Consistent faith in myself. I was never afraid of disappointing anyone as much as you. Not my teachers, not my father, not Scribners or Random House, not even myself . . . just you.

Josie: If that's what you think I'm doing, Ray, I'm so sorry. Clemma said to me today she thought I was missing harmony in my life. Is that what you think?

Ray: I don't know. I never heard you sing.

Josie: Count your lucky stars. Well, I don't want to put any pressure on you, Ray. I want only the best for you but what I want should never be your concern. If we're not right for each other, then I'll accept that. . . .

Ray: I didn't say we weren't right for each other.

Josie (*moves toward him*): Okay. I'll accept that too. But I don't want you or me to rush anything. It seems like everyone here is trying to get their lives straightened out all on this weekend. Why do you think that is?

Ray: It's the end of the summer. Summer is magic. Reality usually starts in September. For me it feels like February.

Josie: If you do go to Houston, will you write to me? A postcard will do.

Ray: I'd write to you from the moon. But how about just a phone call from New York?

Josie: Great. That's much closer than Houston.

Ray: How do you say goodbye without really meaning goodbye?

Josie: You don't say anything.

(*They shake hands, look at each other than he pulls her slowly towards him, and they kiss, warmly. During the kiss, Kenny steps quietly out of the bushes. He's been listening*)

Kenny (*says this simply*): I guess I killed the wrong bird.

(*They turn quickly, devastated*)

Josie: Oh, Kenny, no.

Kenny: You stay here, Ray. *I'll* take the job in Houston.

(*He turns to go*)

Ray: Kenny, wait.

Kenny: For what?

Ray: For me to figure out some way to explain this.

Kenny: Oh, you'll come up with it, Ray. What's another few words after nine hundred thousand?

Josie: Kenny, he never betrayed you. Everything he said or did was always with you in mind.

Kenny: You mean he was kissing you just now for *me?* My God, Ray. What devotion. What friendship.

Ray: Josie, let me and Kenny work this out.

Kenny: No. Let her stay. Let her watch how you and *I* work this out. (*He looks around, sees a fair-sized rock, picks it up, and bounces it in his hand*) Careful, Ray. When it comes to throwing rocks, I'm Olympic material.

Ray: If that's what you want to do . . . go ahead.

(*Vinnie and Sammii appear*)

Vinnie: Oh, here you guys are . . . Hey, Ray. Sammii here's got somethin' she wants me to tell you.

Ray: Sammii, stay back. Kenny has a rock.

(*She runs behind a tree*)

Vinnie (*seeing the problem*): Oh! What do we got here? Daniel and Goliath?

Kenny (*to Ray*): Can you believe, Ray. I actually thought it was Vinnie and Josie. (*To Vinnie*) Good news, Vinnie. You're not the dumbest guy here. I am.

Vinnie: Oh, so *that's* it. Ray's moved in on your girl, heh?

Sammii: Is that true, Ray? I thought you and *I* were going together.

Vinnie (*to Sammii*): This would be a good time to tell him it's over, honey.

Ray: Kenny, put it down. Someone around here is going to get hurt.

Kenny: Worse than me? I don't think so . . . I'll tell you why. Josie I *hoped* for. But you I depended on . . . I would have bet my life on you. You see this rock, Ray? This is our friendship. Well, the *hell* with it.

(*He heaves it into the woods, over their heads*)

Sammii (*screams*): Oh, Jeez, I bet he got another bird.

(*Kenny turns and leaves into the woods*)

Ray: I'm going after him, Josie. Let's put everything on hold for a while, okay?

(*Burt suddenly appears from the other side. He is out of breath*)

Burt: I heard a scream. What happened?

Vinnie: It was like ancient Rome. A fight between two gladiolas.

Josie: Are you alright, Dad?

Burt: I'm fine. Your mother's inside packing. Walter's landing in New York tonight. She promised she'd talk to you before she left. Would you, Josie?

Josie: Mother's ever impeccable timing for leaving.

Burt: And ask Lewis if I could see him for a minute. Nothing urgent.

Josie (*to Vinnie*): Vinnie. I'm sorry. I think it's better if we skip our talk.

Vinnie: It's okay. We're goin' too. I'm gonna drop Sammii off in New York—for a few days—I have a little package for you. Just a trifle.

Josie: Thanks. I love trifles. Shall I open it now?

Vinnie: Don't.

Josie: Well, thanks. Goodbye, Sammii.

(*She rushes into the house*)

Vinnie: Well, we gotta go . . . I hope you don't mind my bustin' in unexpectedly. I just wanted to show my gratitude for somethin' Josie did for me one night in Miami.

Burt: You don't have to tell me what it was.

(*They shake*)

Vinnie (*stands on hill, turns, looks back*): One day I hope to find a place in the woods just like this . . . only on the beach in Miami.

(*He turns and he and Sammii go. As they go, Lewis comes out of the house*)

Lewis: Mr. Hines, Josie said you wanted to see me.

Burt: Unless you're busy.

Lewis: Nothin' that can't wait for you, Mr. Hines. What can I do for you?

Burt: I wonder if you can drive my car for me.

Lewis: I sure can. Want me to go on an errand?

Burt: Well, I thought I'd like to go for a ride . . . you remember where the hospital is, don't you, Lewis?

(*Lewis looks at him stunned*)

(*Music during change.*)

ACT II

Scene Four

It is night. We see Clemma as we saw her at the beginning of the play, sitting on the steps, her sweater wrapped around her to ward off the cold.

Clemma (*out front*): Well . . . That man had himself another heart attack and I never speculated on what brought it on. He pulled out of it and came back to finish the summer like he planned. But it was his last summer. He passed away in his sleep, middle of November of that year . . . and it took me some time before I realized I had just lost a family . . . Mrs. *Robbins* had her new husband, Mr. Hines was gone and didn' need a cook and Josie had grown past needin' a nanny. And I was a free woman . . . which is what all the young people of my color was shoutin' about then. Our civil rights . . . and it was about time. It confused me at first 'cause the Hines family was always civil to me and to my way of lookin', I was the one who had all the rights in that family, whether they knew it or not. But I moved on in the world . . . Me and Lewis opened a small restaurant in the city, featurin' my cookin' and my puttin' up most of the money . . . But Lewis, true to his word, worked his good hand to the bone and his good heart to death. But we did have twenny-two fine years together . . . and I raised a niece and two nephews of mine right up through college. (*She gets up*) But as I said before, on nights like this, my mind goes back to this house, this time of year . . . and in particular, to the last night of that summer when we packed to close it up . . . not knowin' it would be for the last time.

(*Lewis and Burt come up from one of the paths. Burt is walking slowly, leaning on Lewis' arm. Clemma watches this but they don't see her. She's in the future while they're still in the past*)

Lewis: You're doin' real fine, Mr. Hines. I can hardly keep up with you.

Burt: I don't know . . . When that turtle passed me, I knew I was in trouble.

Lewis (*laughs*): Well, you'll be back in the city tomorrow. Be yourself in no time. (*Burt stops, winded. He holds on to the back of a chair*) You want to rest?

Burt: Just a second. (*He looks at porch steps*)

Clemma (*to the audience*): It was the half-blind helping the three-quarters maimed . . . Mrs. Robbins came back for the second time that summer . . . 'cause she sensed there'd never be another.

(*Annie's on the upstairs porch, smoking*)

(*They stop on the downstairs porch to rest*)

Burt: So how are you and Clemma doing? You two going to work it out?

Lewis: Well, hard to say. She's like an apple on an autumn tree. Looks ready to fall but keeps holding to the stem with a powerful grip.

Burt: Don't wait, Lewis. Shake the tree. Chop it down if you have to. But don't leave it up to the apple. There's always someone else ready to pick it off. (*He starts into house*) Okay. Who wants to play gin rummy?

(*Annie goes back in*)

Clemma: Lewis? . . . Lewis.

(*He comes out, stands on the porch*)

Lewis: What I do wrong now?

Clemma: We won't have much time to talk 'cause me and the family's goin' home first thing in the mornin'.

Lewis: I know.

Clemma: I *know* you know. I just want to know what your plans are.

Lewis: I tole you my plans. I'm goin' back to New York, find myself a place to live.

Clemma: Good idea, 'cause I been thinkin', things just ain't gonna work out between you and me.

Lewis: You already tole me that. Why you tellin' me again?

Clemma: 'Cause lately you been showin' signs of losin' your hearin' as well.

Lewis: I hear you the first time. I stop listenin' the second, third, and fifth time.

Clemma: You still plannin' on openin' that restaurant you been talkin' about?

Lewis: Well, I got my eye on a place and I got my eye on someone to cook.

Clemma: I'm just askin'.

Lewis: Clemma, you and Mr. Hines been real nice puttin' me up these few weeks. But I gotta get on with my life. No need to worry 'bout me.

Clemma: I ain't worried 'bout you. Why would I worry about you?

Lewis: Then don't.

(*He goes back into the house. She turns to go back into the kitchen*)

Clemma: I spent seven years not worryin' 'bout him, so I don't need no practice. (*She stops*) He's just workin' on you, Clemma, that's all that man's doin'.

(*Josie comes up the path carrying a heavy set of golf clubs*)

Josie: Who are you talking to, Clemma?

Clemma: No one. I just don' like bein' worked on, tha's all . . . Watcha doin' with your Daddy's clubs?

(*Josie lays the clubs against the bench*)

Josie: When he's feeling better, he might want to go down to Florida, maybe play nine holes. A little optimism never hurt.

113

Clemma: You alright, child?

Josie (*looks at the house, then at Clemma*)**:** My mother's looking for me. To have that "end of summer" talk. Only I can't worry about "our relationship" and "our condition" when she knows my father may not even . . . Why is she here? She can't save his life.

Clemma: No, she can't. And she knows it. It's you and her she's tryin' to save, Josie.

Josie: She had her chance a few years ago when she left. If she didn't, maybe *none* of us would have to be saved.

Clemma: I never said you didn't have a right to be angry with your Momma. No one can go through life without goin' through that feelin'.

Josie: But she wants me to forgive her for *everything.* And she never forgave my father for being away so much.

Clemma: It ain't my place to judge 'em, Josie.

Josie: Well, maybe you were lucky. You told me there never was a divorce in your family.

Clemma: Tha's right. 'Cause my Daddy died when I was twelve years old. My momma didn't have time to be angry at her loss 'cause she had seven children to raise . . . So I got angry for her.

Josie: With who?

Clemma: With God. And let me tell you, girl, that takin' on your mother ain't *nothin'* to takin' on God . . . You get fresh with the Lord, He can puff you right out of the universe . . . But I took him on anyway.

Josie: What did you do?

Clemma: I went to church but I didn't say my prayers to Him. And that's when my momma taught me about anger. She said to me, "Clemma, if you got anger in your heart, you get rid of it fast. 'Cause anger with no place to go, looks for a place to settle, and can make a real comfortable home inside of you to last out your life." I don't care how strong you are, girl, no one can carry that weight around for a lifetime and be happy. You understand, Josie?

Josie: Except for one thing. You had brothers and sisters to share your anger with. I'm all alone in this. Maybe it's why I grabbed onto Kenny because at least he'd be there for me . . . And there was you. I've always had you, Clemma. If my mother never gave me anything else in life, I thank God she gave me you.

Clemma (*she's hurt by this*): I ain't a thing to give, Josie. I'm a woman who needed a job and I was real glad to get this one 'cause they don't come easy.

Josie: Oh, God, Clemma, I didn't mean it to sound like that.

Clemma: I know you didn't. And I didn't know I was gonna come to love you so much . . . I always treated you like you was my child, Josie but you ain't my child . . . Because there's no blood between us. That's somethin' only you can have with your momma.

Josie: Then why couldn't she talk to me the way you are now?

Clemma: 'Cause you never gave her the chance. When your daddy goes, Josie, there won't be no place in your life for me. And all summer long I could see that day was comin' soon . . . You and me's gonna have to say goodbye, honey.

Josie: No we won't. I'll always see you, Clemma. Always.

Clemma: Maybe. But we don't need each other like we once did. You only have one real mother, Josie. Don't squander it . . . So you forgive her and you forgive your Daddy.

Josie: Forgive him for what?

Clemma: For not bein' here when you was growin' up . . . and your mother *was* here for you, wasn't she?

Josie: Yes, but—

Clemma: *Wasn't*, she, Josie?

Josie: Yes.

(*Annie comes out*)

Annie: I thought I heard you out here.

Clemma: Oh, 'scuse me, Mrs. Robbins. I was just goin' in to help Lewis with the packin'.

(*She looks at Josie, reaches out and touches her hand, then goes into the house*)

Annie: Josie—

Josie: Mom, could—could we just skip it for tonight. I will do it, I promise. Tomorrow or the day after. Could we?

Annie: We can't keep putting it off forever, Josie. I can't deal one more minute with this—this hatred you have for me.

Josie: I don't hate you, mother. I was angry before, yes. But I need something else right now that you can't give me.

Annie: What's that?

Josie: I'm not ready for him to go yet. I don't want this to be his last summer. I don't want to close up this house tonight and never be able to see him sitting in that chair, warming himself in the sun, and thinking how great it once was. When we were a family.

Annie: Nobody can give you that, Josie.

Josie: I *know* that. And I will love you again. I promise. Do you think I could go through burying him without you to hold on to? But somehow this silly little child in me is still hoping for a happy ending. That you'd leave Walter and come back to Dad. And we'd all have one last summer again. It's not going to happen, I know that. But I don't have to know it tonight. Tonight. That's all I'm talking about.

Annie: I understand. I do. Oh, Josie, I just want to put my arms around you and make it alright. But I can wait. I'll wait as long as you want, sweetheart.

Josie (*bursts into tears, throws arms around her mother*)**:** I love you. I really do, Mom. I just wish it would get better right away.

Annie: I know. I know, baby . . . Shh, it's alright. I'm here for you . . . I'll always be here for you.

(*They hold each other. Burt appears on the upper balcony*)

Burt (*he watches a moment, then*)**:** Annie? I can't find that cashmere sweater you gave me for my birthday. . . .

Annie (*looks up*)**:** Burt, you shouldn't have climbed those stairs.

Burt: You're absolutely right . . . Come up and give me your shoulder to lean on.

(*He smiles at her. Annie looks at Josie. Josie smiles and nods. Annie goes into the house*)

Josie (*looks up*)**:** Dad . . .

Burt: I wasn't listening . . . But thank you, baby . . . Thank you.

(*He throws her a kiss and goes back in. Josie turns around, a look of great relief on her face. Ray walks on*)

Ray: Josie . . . Hi.

Josie (*turns, surprised*): Hi. I thought you were in New York, working.

Ray: I am. I took a coffee break and drove ninety miles to see you. . . .

Josie: You have a glint in your eye.

Ray: No, it's the reflection of the moon. You have to position yourself right.

Josie: Have you seen Kenny?

Ray: Oh, yeah. He's fine about you. Fine about me. He's not ready to give me blood again, but he's okay. How's your father?

Josie: I'm keeping my fingers crossed . . . (*She tilts her head*) No, it's not the moon. You have a definite glint in your eye.

Ray: I confess. I have some good news. Someone wants to publish my book. A small new company in Seattle.

Josie: Oh, Ray. That's wonderful.

Ray: I turned them down. I thanked them and said maybe next year. I heard you in my head saying, "Not yet, Ray. Don't rush it. Do it when it's right."

Josie: God, I missed you. (*She starts to move towards him, he holds up his arm to block her*)

Ray: I have a small present for you.

(*He holds it out. She takes it*)

Josie: Really? First thing you've ever given me.

Ray: Open it . . .

(*She looks at it. She rips off the paper. It's a thin bound book*)

Josie: Leather bound?

Ray: Imitation. It's the thought of the price that counts.

(*She opens it, then thumbs through the pages*)

Josie: A book of blank pages?

Ray: Except for the dedication. (*He points to the right page*)

Josie (*reads*): "To Josie . . . these are the pages of our lives together, to be filled in as they reveal themselves . . . You are a most fortunate woman in having won the heart of a truly remarkable man, who finally feels he's worthy of you."

(*She looks at him, filled with emotion*)

Ray: Let me finish it (*He takes the book from her and reads it*) "Though the world will soon beat a path to my doorway, the house will be empty. I will be otherwise occupied with a friend writing post-cards from the moon . . . Okay, so it's a little flowery, but— (*She kisses him before he can finish. He looks up*) Thank God. A good review.

Josie: Don't drive back tonight.

Ray: I wasn't. Kenny gave me the keys to his house.

Josie: What's wrong with *my* house?

Ray: Your parents are here. And Lewis and Clemma.

Josie: No one would mind. Or even notice. I don't know if we'll ever come back here. It would make me happy to know that everyone I care about is sleeping in this house tonight.

(*He leans over, kisses her*)

Ray: I'll go help with the bags. (*Points to the book*) Hold onto this. It's a First Edition.

(*He leaves. Annie comes out of the house, looks towards the lake*)

Annie: You'd never know he had a heart attack three weeks ago. Every time I go in there, he's beaming and smiling. What's he so happy about?

Josie: That tonight feels like it used to be.

(*Clemma comes out*)

Clemma: Well, I guess no one needs me with Lewis and your young man doin' all the heavy work . . . which is why God thought up men in the first place.

Annie (*looks up*): I can't remember the sky ever being this clear. Can you, Josie?

Josie (*looks up*): Yes, Mom. Ever since we've been coming up here.

Annie: I suppose you're right.

Clemma: Look at them birds over there just waitin' for us to get out so they can get all the leftovers in the bins.

Annie: When Josie was a girl, she always made sure I left plenty of food outside when we left . . . for the animals to get through the winter . . . I used to see squirrels running up into the trees carrying Oreo cookies.

Josie: I wonder what it's going to be like up here in a hundred years.

Clemma: Well, you just come back and find out.

Josie: I'll be long gone in a hundred years, Clemma.

Clemma: May be . . . but that's no reason to stop you from coming back.

(*They all look out, into the night*)

(*Dim out. Curtain*)